The Purpose-Driven Organization

Perry Pascarella
Mark A. Frohman

The Purpose-Driven Organization

Unleashing the Power of
Direction and Commitment

 Jossey-Bass Publishers
San Francisco • Oxford • 1990

THE PURPOSE-DRIVEN ORGANIZATION
Unleashing the Power of Direction and Commitment
by Perry Pascarella and Mark A. Frohman

Copyright © 1989 by: Jossey-Bass Inc., Publishers
350 Sansome Street
San Francisco, California 94104

Jossey-Bass Limited
Headington Hill Hall
Oxford OX3 0BW

Perry Pascarella
30413 Winsor Drive
Bay Village, Ohio 44140

Mark A. Frohman
8240 Stoney Brook Drive
Chagrin Falls, Ohio 44022

Library of Congress Cataloging-in-Publication Data

Pascarella, Perry.
    The purpose-driven organization : unleashing the power of
direction and commitment / Perry Pascarella, Mark A. Frohman. — 1st
ed.
      p. cm. — (The Jossey-Bass management series)
    Bibliography: p.
    Includes index.
    ISBN 1-55542-176-8 (alk. paper)
    1. Organizational effectiveness. 2. Organizational change.
I. Frohman, Mark A., date. II. Title. III. Series.
HD58.9.P37 1989
658.4'063—dc20   89-45591
                                               CIP

Manufactured in the United States of America

The paper in this book meets the guidelines for
permanence and durability of the Committee on
Production Guidelines for Book Longevity of
the Council on Library Resources.

Credits are on page 179.

FIRST EDITION
    First printing: October 1989
    Second printing: July 1990

Code 8950

*The Jossey-Bass
Management Series*

To our wives, Carol and Sue,
who have given us extraordinary reason
for purposefulness and passion.
And to our children,
Cindy, Betsy, Scott, and Gregg,
who expanded our limits of managing change
while we were wishing for stability.

Contents

Preface

Executives and managers at all levels face two difficult tasks. First, in order for organizations to survive, leaders must manage both stability and change. How do leaders know when to reinforce the routine and when to encourage innovation? Second, people want both to be effective as individuals and to find meaning in their lives at work. How can leaders help bring this about?

The Purpose-Driven Organization argues that any organization concerned about its future needs to define its purpose in order to address both of these problems. Organizations need to define where they are going and what they stand for in order to achieve organizational viability and encourage employee commitment.

Through our exposure to many organizations we have seen executives working with individual pieces of this puzzle—such as employee participation, a mission statement, or a strategic plan. Some have put several pieces together. But these are examples of micromanagement. We believe there is a much bigger picture to be seen. We are convinced that what leaders need is a frame of reference that can guide their assembling the pieces into a meaningful whole. Leaders have to become macromanagers in order to determine when to preserve what they have accomplished and when to support new processes and techniques.

We see a form of organization emerging that brings together some of the best organizational and managerial techniques and lifts them to a new stage of organizational growth. This new organization defines its purpose and makes that central to all its policies and activities. It provides both memory of what has been worthwhile in the past and a vision of what can be in the future. Profit has been likened to the lifeblood of a corporation; profit is not why a corporation lives but what keeps it alive. We think of purpose as the reason for an organization's existence.

Why We Wrote This Book

The existing literature provides little or no guidance to enable top executives to fulfill their principal responsibility— providing a sense of purpose and creating an environment that will develop and support a sense of responsibility in other people. *The Purpose-Driven Organization* addresses the gap between visionary leadership and results; visionary leadership alone is not enough. Organizations need a framework that permits the processes, procedures, systems, and organizational nuts and bolts to be integrated and in tune with one another.

We want *The Purpose-Driven Organization* to be both inspirational and instructional. We want to coax and then coach management to create the more effective, competitive organizations that people and conditions demand. We wrote this book because we want to see organizations and individuals fulfilled and achieving the best they can. While we have much experience of "what is," we have an even stronger desire to pave the way for "what can be."

Intended Audience

The Purpose-Driven Organization is directed to executives and middle managers in business organizations and to others who want to run businesslike organizations. Most leaders recognize that some things need to change and others need to remain unchanged; but they do not know what to change, how far to go, or where to begin. Those who have tried their hand at writing a mission statement, practicing participative management, or changing corporate culture should find our observations and suggestions useful. This book provides down-to-earth help in executing some of these new ideas within a broader context that we call *purpose*.

Overview of the Contents

The Purpose-Driven Organization describes a model for the philosophy and practices that can help an organization attain a new stage of effectiveness. Crucial to this model is the development of a meaningful statement of corporate purpose, which provides a reference point to guide continual improvement and increased competitiveness.

In the first two chapters, we discuss how an overarching purpose meets both corporate and personal needs. Then, in Chapters Three and Four, we address the nuts-and-bolts issues involved in writing and communicating a purpose statement—the first steps in becoming a purpose-driven organization. Chapter Five describes for executives how purpose enhances both the planning process and plan implementation. In Chapter Six, we describe how to establish a tracking system that measures how well the organization's performance matches its purpose statement. In the next chapter, we explain how purpose sets the stage for the innovation-seeking organization to determine what to change and what not to change, at the same time unleashing people's commitment.

The final three chapters deal with purpose-driven leadership. Chapter Eight describes how leaders take a stand and champion actions consistent with the corporate purpose. We show in Chapter Nine how this foundation enables leaders to deal with the increasing complexities and paradoxes that confront them by employing intuitive as well as scientific management practices. In Chapter Ten, we provide examples of how leaders manage the decision-making process in ways that enable others to support the purpose. The resource provides a way to measure progress toward becoming a purpose-driven organization; it provides 131 sample questions for surveying stakeholders inside and outside the organization.

Acknowledgments

We are in debt to many people in our professional and personal lives who have given us ideas and impetus for *The Purpose-Driven Organization*. Although these people have played diverse roles—clients, writers, consultants, executives in every conceivable type of organization—all have been our teachers. We take this opportunity to express our appreciation to each of them. We hope they look favorably on our work, which has been shaped by their influence.

We pay special thanks to four people. Alan Frohman, more than any other person, had a significant and valued impact on our thinking and writing. His emphasis on helping managers identify issues and pull strategy into action is reflected in several of our chapters. Dan Keegan helped us sort out and then integrate many of the bits and pieces of our experiences in the areas of planning, strategy setting, and performance reporting. Vincent DiBianca helped us to develop an appreciation of the power of possibility and to distinguish the marks of leadership. Frederick Herzberg taught us that to be effective at work is a basic need for being human. His ability to bridge the realities of the workplace and the values by which we live in his many writings gave us guidance for our own work.

To one another, we acknowledge that "coauthors" does not do justice to the rich exchange of ideas and mental leap-frogging we experienced. We have shared purpose, passion, and fun in writing together.

Cleveland, Ohio   Perry Pascarella
July 1989   Mark A. Frohman

The Authors

Perry Pascarella was elected vice-president–editorial of Penton Publishing Company in 1989. Prior to that he was editor-in-chief of the company's well-known *Industry Week* magazine. Pascarella received an A.B. degree (1956) in English from Kenyon College. He has studied industry management here and abroad for more than twenty-five years. His extensive writings have made him a sought-after speaker, lecturer, and seminar leader. He has collaborated with such celebrated management experts as Peter Drucker, Frederick Herzberg, and Thomas Peters. He is particularly noted for his visionary work in humanistic and participative management and in managing change.

Pascarella has written three future-oriented books on organizations and society: *Technology—Fire in a Dark World* (1979), *Humanagement in the Future Corporation* (1980), and *The New Achievers* (1984).

The American Society of Business Press Editors has recognized Pascarella's work with awards for editorial and feature writing. He is a member of the National Association of Business Economists, the World Future Society, the American Teilhard Association for the Future of Man, the advisory council of the Institute for Future Studies at the University of Akron, and the Ohio Scanning Network.

Mark A. Frohman, president of Organization Resources, is a consultant to numerous large and small corporations on managing organizational growth, productivity, innovation, team-building, and strategy implementation. His extensive experience with top executives and senior-level managers in industrial and service firms in the United States and abroad has made him a valued adviser on strategy and action issues. For fifteen years prior to forming his own consulting firm he gained valuable experience in senior positions in several organizations.

While in industry, Frohman's work in improving productivity, teamwork, and profitability received attention in the national media, including American Management Association publications and *Industry Week*.

Frohman received his B.A. degree (1966) in psychology from the University of Rochester and his M.A. (1968) and Ph.D. (1970) degrees in organizational psychology from the University of Michigan, where his work concentrated on strategies of organization change. He has published numerous articles on methods of diagnosing and solving organization problems, managing for growth, and participative management. To remain a "practitioner," he is very active as a board member of several community organizations.

The Purpose-Driven Organization

Chapter 1

Dynamics of a Purpose-Driven Organization

There ought to be a better way to get the job done. And there is. There always is.

From time to time, established business organizations modify their structures and their systems of controls and rewards in order to improve performance and become more competitive. They go through periods of centralizing operations and then decentralizing. They realign divisions and departments. They establish new staffs of specialists, task forces, and study groups. They adjust compensation systems. In general, they constantly seek better ways to maintain continuity and control because they are established, in the first place, to reinforce certain ways of doing things.

In this new age of competition and sweeping change, the typical business organization needs something beyond modification. It needs not just one-time change but also the flexibility that will enable it to change continually to improve quality and productivity if it is to compete. It has to be open to innovation in every activity and at every level. To continually improve the value of its products and services and the effectiveness of its processes for producing and delivering them, the organization needs employees capable of promoting and providing innovation in its own design and style.

Three major rivers of change are converging on the corporation, forcing it toward a significant transformation that will enable it to respond to change now and forcing it to establish

1

a change-making process able to deal with the future's unknowns.

1. The marketplace is now global. Fewer and fewer companies can escape the likelihood of facing foreign competitors. More and more are turning to foreign suppliers to help them reduce costs or create other competitive advantages. Some companies are awakening to the sales potential in foreign markets. In recent years, some have discovered a new reality of the global economy: the acquisition of their company or their vendors or customers by foreign firms. The power of this globalization of business is of a magnitude greater than that of the colonization that crept slowly through the world during earlier centuries. It is happening faster, affecting more people, and creating constant shifting in the relative standing among industrialized nations. This change continually raises the number of potential competitors in any product line or market.

2. Technology is advancing at an accelerating pace and quickly flows throughout the world. Overnight, a new technology can change what a company makes, how it makes it, and who its competitors are. New technology thereby can change the type of people and organizations needed to make effective use of it. The world is experiencing a period of high innovation. When and if the pace will subside no one knows, but even if this era were to end today, many existing technologies that have not fully worked their way across the economy would continue to affect business for years to come.

3. Over the past quarter century, there has been an explosion of new values and life-styles. Mixed with the old, they have created staggering diversity that makes old assumptions about the roles people play as producers and consumers obsolete. Through both roles, people are expressing their values as they demand that more attention be paid to quality. Quality has many aspects such as the basic feature of a product, serviceability, esthetics, reputation of the producer, and ease of purchase. Different aspects may appeal to different potential customers. In addition, customers' wants, their perceptions of the products offered, or the criteria by which they judge products may change over time. Quality, an elusive target, demands continual change.

While the times call for change, major organizational change threatens the very people with the central role in operating our organizations. Managers are appointed to keep things running. Although many of them like to think of themselves as agents of change, they often regard innovation merely as an add-on—something to create enough headway to keep the corporate ship from drifting into danger. They overlook the other ships bearing down on them. All too often, managers perceive change as endangering their organization and their place in it. When top executives try to bring about major change, they then meet heavy resistance from their own management teams. Senior executives are caught between the external signals calling for change and the internal resistance to it.

Managers generally are receptive to specific new programs or techniques that promise to tune up the existing organization without endangering its basic design. These piecemeal efforts, however, may not address the most serious challenges a particular organization faces. Or they may not address the new conditions confronting the organization with sufficient force to really help. If managers blindly adopt new techniques or programs, they can damage the existing organization with ideas that are incompatible with ongoing operations. They are unlikely to create a net gain if they do not implement new programs within a framework that enhances the overall organization and its competitive position. A company may, for example, go overboard in cost reduction and injure its long-term health, or it may focus its improvement efforts on the marketing department to the detriment of other departments.

Many executives now recognize the need to redefine their concept of organizational effectiveness and what structure and style they need to make their organizations more effective. Many of them are searching for ways to bring their organizations in tune with the outside world and elicit information and insights from more and more members of their work force.

Many executives have witnessed the value of drawing upon the creativity and commitment of people throughout the organization. In some manufacturing companies, middle managers, engineers, and even blue-collar workers are visiting customers' factories to study the reaction to their present products and look for needs that might be met with future products. These companies recognize that the marketing department cannot do the marketing job alone and that the sales department cannot effectively handle the selling effort working in isolation from other departments.

These organizations now stand at the threshold between tinkering and substantial change. Their top executives sense that something needs to be done either to change the corporate culture or solidify recent changes in it. The new pressures on them and the capabilities that they are discovering in their employees point to the need for a framework that will enable senior executives to select the best from old and new management techniques and create an effective balance between stability and change. They want to support the new processes and techniques that have opened their organizations to change and cooperation. They are willing to give up some control in exchange for lasting commitment to the good accomplishments in recent years. They have seen that enthusiasm for a quality circle process can peak out in two or three years. They have found that broad quality improvement programs eventually lose momentum; they then search for ways to rededicate the organization to quality.

Some corporate cultures have been changed unintentionally as new techniques were adopted. Despite the lack of agreement about what corporate culture is, some executives are trying to deliberately alter it by wrestling with such concepts as teamwork, values, vision, and mission. There is little point in building teamwork, however, unless the team knows what it is working toward—where the total organization is going. Mission statements also are of little value in the absence of a fully conceived management program that supports the corporate mission in every aspect of corporate activity and wins commitment.

Grand Convergence of Trends

The convergence of a number of seemingly unrelated developments is not only creating the need for fundamental change in today's organization but also offers the means of attaining it. An organization can begin restructuring itself by building on advances that have already broken with tradition.

For more than a decade, managers increasingly have paid attention to participative management and employee involvement. At the upper levels of organizations, these processes are breaking down the rigidities of traditional planning techniques as executives view setting and implementing strategies as creative, participative processes. At all levels, employees are being readied for operating with greater self-reliance in a trend that calls for both increased independence and increased coordination.

Many of the managers now rising to the upper ranks have a new view of the world and of people; they see more potential in individuals and operate in a style that demands that people use their talents to the fullest degree and enables them to develop and exercise those talents. They have been closer to the action than have those who wielded the hierarchical controls of the past. They are results oriented, and they know that they cannot get the results they need without the help of others.

Computer-based technologies enable management to pull together many formerly disparate activities and functions; this promotes far more decentralized activity without a loss of coordination.

In many cases, internal and external forces have led to restructuring organizations and flattening their multilayered hierarchies. Some established companies have cut their layers of management from twelve to eight. In their plants, they have cut the number of echelons from seven to five. Start-up plants sometimes have as few as one or two layers of management.

Cost reductions have pruned away staff specialists and thrust a broader range of planning, analysis, and policy-setting responsibilities on line management.

More companies are turning outward in corporate focus. American management lost sight of the importance of quality for years as it concentrated on growth in sales volume. Producers established standards of acceptability from their own viewpoint rather than that of their customers. During the early 1980s, heavy concentration on productivity improvement tended to draw attention still further away from the customer; efforts directed inward to cost reduction often detracted from quality. By the mid eighties, a fundamental shift had begun. Executives no longer see quality as a matter of conforming to internal specifications; instead, they consider the customer. This represents a profound shift in attitude. Jerry Junkins, chairman of Texas Instruments, warns: "If you don't look out, . . . you will tend to optimize around your internal organization and force your customers to adapt to your organization, because—theoretically—it makes *you* more efficient." He says you should, instead, be working to make your customer more efficient (Sheridan, 1988, p. 67).

Time for a New Model

Managers have difficulty visualizing where pressures and recent progress are taking today's organization. They need a new model for the business organization because the ones with which they are familiar suggest that their organizations will eventually become so bound up in internal structures that they will lose their vitality. They are determined to break through to new ground to reshape their organizations' competitiveness.

The typical models relate to the stages of organizational development: start-up, growth, and maturity. An entrepreneur launches a *start-up* company—Stage One—by doing nearly everything, including designing the product, financing the business, lining up customers, and delivering the goods. Risk is high in this stage. The organizational structure is flat. Even as the firm grows and the owner hires help, roles and responsibilities remain loosely defined. The entrepreneur plans and controls the company while he or she gradually assigns operating duties to others. Overall, the style is one of individualism, informal relationships, and close attention to marketplace success.

If the start-up organization succeeds, it then evolves into the *growth stage* as the entrepreneur adds employees, equipment, and control methods. Hierarchy and division of labor become more pronounced in Stage Two. Personal relationships give way to job definitions and formal reporting systems. Management, looking to gain control of the mushrooming organization, starts to rely on more formal procedures. It initiates standards and automation to improve efficiency. Close contact between the owner and customers may diminish and be replaced by the introduction of more formal marketing and sales functions. The threat of failure decreases in Stage Two because the organization has acquired a stable business base. At the same time, management's tendency to avoid risk rises, thereby leading the business toward the next stage of development.

The *mature company*—Stage Three—slows in growth because of increasing competition or a changed environment. Growth makes necessary complex budgeting and planning systems and substantial increases in staff to handle administrative and reporting requirements and the greater volume of business. With the slowdown in growth and the increased investment in structure comes a low-risk propensity. Managers strive for stability and control to improve results; therefore they focus on strengthening the planning process and control systems.

The orientation toward stability and control of a Stage Three organization develops through its adaptation to a history of growth; an environment that has been fairly predictable in political, legal, economic, and technological changes; and its position in a marketplace characterized by familiar and nonvolatile competition. When such growth and stability supports disappear, the organization becomes an enemy unto itself. The stability of Stage Three can turn into stagnation as management becomes uncertain about which technology to invest in; spends too much time perfecting old technology, obsolete equipment, and products; develops more layers of hierarchy; slows its decision-making process; avoids risk; and isolates itself from the customer. In Stage Three companies, managers tend to spend too much time guessing what the corporation should be doing and then second-guessing what it has done. They tend to focus on activities rather than on results; because there is no meaningful basis for evaluating results, activity takes on a value of its own.

Prolonged maturity leads to rigidity and, sometimes, rigor mortis. In mature companies, management sometimes attempts to loosen the system, struggling to reenergize the organization by trying to restore the informality and togetherness employees once had (perhaps beyond the recall of anyone now in the company). Managers would like to somehow recapture the excitement and spirit of some earlier stage in the company's development. They assume that what they need is a little more of Stage One, if not a return to the simplicity and freshness of it. They urge workers to be more entrepreneurial and sometimes establish entrepreneurial units within the rigid overall structure.

A return to an earlier stage is neither sufficient nor necessary—even if it were possible—to lead a mature company onward. *Onward* is a key word. Although some of the prescriptions for remedying organizational ills would replicate some aspects of earlier stages of organizational development, most organizations are ill equipped to go backward even if they really wanted to. Rather than regarding the mature organization as the final stage of development, management should consider the possibility of a fourth stage in organizational life. Let us call it the *purpose-driven organization*.

Some companies have moved out of Stage Three and need a better model with which to identify themselves. Transition to a fourth stage would be a continuation of their evolutionary process as they adapt to their changing environment and to the changing internal forces that have made doing business the old way ineffective. Other companies, in Stage One or Two, could avoid the stagnation that they fear will inevitably overtake them. An organization driven by purpose can override the tendencies to become complacent and stagnant. Purpose can provide the vitality, direction, and flexibility so often lacking in business organizations. Purpose can help set limits for the organization so it can focus its strengths and resources on its best products, markets, and opportunities.

An organization becomes truly purpose driven by capturing the sense of purpose that a leader provides, institutionalizing it, and making it the driving force for all of the organization's activities, policies, and practices. Then members of the organization can clearly understand the purpose, make a commitment to it, and live by it. A clearly stated purpose expresses the values and core beliefs of the organization's members. That purpose will set the direction for what the organization wants to accomplish and provide guidance for implementation. We envision this as yet uncharted fourth stage of organizational development emerging as the model for the organization that will take us into the twenty-first century. (See Table 1.) The following chapters describe this model and the elements of a purpose-driven organization. It is a model that can broaden the horizons for a company in any of the three conventional stages.

Crystalizing a Purpose

We can already see the features of a purpose-driven organization in some companies. In the past decade, significant changes in structure, management style, and delegation of authority have reached the heart of the organization. The new possibilities for the structure and spirit of business organizations that we can now see emerging strongly suggest that we are on the threshold of a new era. Many chief executives are searching for a definition of their company's purpose or mission. Others have a clear sense of their organization's purpose, but they lack the techniques for incorporating it into management practices and support systems to bring it to life. All these executives are struggling to reestablish their organizations on the basis of business goals and personal values that will draw all members of the organization into a commitment to continually improve effectiveness. They venture out alone because there is little theory or experience to guide them. They are led only by their own need for purpose-driven action.

The first step in creating a purpose-driven organization is determining clearly what that unique purpose is. Then top management writes a statement of purpose. The purpose statement defines the line of business in terms general enough to allow for flexibility and growth yet specific enough to guide the organization's members in their daily operations. It describes the arena of action. It sets limits, stating how the organization will act and for whose benefit it is acting.

Table 1. Characteristics of the Purpose-Driven Organization.

	Typical Mature Organization	Purpose-Driven Organization
Use of Purpose	Limited sloganism	Drives all activities
Operations	Stable	Exploration of alternatives
Top Management Style	Watchdog Hierarchical	Purposeful, visionary, participative
Management Focus	Improving the pieces	Conveying vision and context
Willingness to Risk	Low	Moderate
Planning	Formal, structured	Formal, informal, flexible
Tracking	Accounting based	Strategy based
Measurements	Quantitative	Quantitative and qualitative
Innovation Type	Incremental product and process improvement	Breakthroughs and incremental improvements
	Departmental	Everyone's province
Communications	Structured	Formal and informal, networks
Control	Procedures, rules	Purpose, self-discipline
Rewards	Not tied to plans	Linked to plans
Customer Relations	We/they	Partnerships, alliances

Writing *mission statements* that describe a company's business objectives was popular in the mid eighties. *Corporate credos* that express a code of ethics have been around much longer. Peter Block describes still another corporate document: the *vision statement*. While a mission statement describes what business we are in, a vision statement ''is an expression of hope''—a vision ''of how we would like the organization to be,'' he says (1987, p. 107).

We use the term *purpose statement* as a reminder that an effective statement has to incorporate the essential elements of all three types of statements just cited. It must state not only the line or lines of business but also the values that employees, owners, customers, and others with a stake in the organization will support. Description of the business activity is important because people need to know what will make the organization effective in the marketplace, and they need human values to give them a goal—something they can be loyal to. Together these expressions of intent serve as the foundation for corporate policies, systems, decision-making processes, and individual behavior. While some existing corporate statements may meet these criteria, their respective organizations should determine that this is, in fact, the case. We also feel that the term *purpose* implies something more compelling—something more fundamental to the organization than *mission.* Purpose is not simply a target that an organization chooses to aim for; it is the organization's reason for being.

The top management of an organization can establish an appropriate purpose only after carefully considering what it wants to accomplish, how it wants to balance short- and long-term priorities, and to what employees in the organization will commit their personal energy. The setting of purpose therefore requires self-examination and an examination of the marketplace. This collaborative, arduous process creates a model of a dynamic organization that people can serve boldly and with pride.

Expressing purpose in a written statement calls for balancing a number of seemingly paradoxical factors. As Thomas Peters (1987, p. 401) observes, "Developing a vision and values is a messy, artistic process." A statement of purpose must deal, for example, with both the present and the future because the strategy that will be based on the purpose will need to optimize ongoing operational activities as well as leave room for the new and unplanned. A purpose statement must convey both the important qualitative and quantitative dimensions of organizational life: It needs to express what the organization wants to accomplish in providing value to its stakeholders—owners, employees, customers, vendors, and the public—and describe how those accomplishments can be measured.

The statement of purpose attends not only to the organization itself but also to all its stakeholders so they can readily understand how they receive value from this organization directly or indirectly. Just as individuals need to make a commitment to something larger than themselves, so does the organization. The organization is not an end in itself; it serves some larger purpose. "Organization purpose is not simply decided by its members, but is in large part 'given' by its membership in the larger system," Roger Harrison (1983, p. 223) reminds us. Each group with a stake in an organization will judge its effectiveness. For this reason, the purpose statement must contain elements that are directed toward others. It may start by relating to the value the customer will receive. From there the writers of the purpose statement work their way through the rewards—financial and nonfinancial—that other interested parties will receive when the customer is served.

One major consulting firm clearly describes its line of business, the factors for measuring success, and—not so incidentally—its employees: "We strive to be the pre-eminent firm providing financial, planning and control, and information technology services to large industrial and service companies. We strive to have an impact on the economic future of those companies and on the economy as a whole. We strive to provide services with a top management orientation, dealing directly with key decision makers in each client. We strive to maintain and advance our leadership role in manufacturing/cost management. We strive to achieve pre-eminence through the acquisition of superior people and the development of a superior staff. We strive to achieve pre-eminence as measured by . . ."

An automotive components supplier does a skillful job of blending financial and nonfinancial factors to present its purpose to members of the organization. It states that it is committed to: "1. Serving customers by providing creative design, innovative engineering and efficient manufacture of products that set the standards for quality and value leadership; 2. Promoting a work environment characterized by high expectations, active involvement, open communications, and trusting relationships; 3. Earning a return on investment sufficient to meet responsibilities to stockholders, to each other, to family and to the community; 4. Sharing our corporate financial success by allocating maximum charitable contributions to be used for those institutions or causes deserving our assistance and support."

One large manufacturing company's statement sets high standards covering additional considerations: "We're in the electronics instrument business, using measurements to meet the needs of our customers in research and design throughout the world. We want to be a rapidly growing company that is the industry leader in shareholders' equity and return on sales. We want to provide opportunity and satisfaction for our people based upon their individual creativity and performance. We want to be the best in what we do and strive to be the technological leader in those areas in which we choose to concentrate. We want to be famous for our level of quality and service."

As these examples show, a purpose statement can deal squarely with both financial and nonfinancial considerations. They address financial objectives in a way that permits members to see how they can contribute to the organization's financial success. A statement may explain too how financial success will enable the organization to serve nonfinancial values that may be equally or more important to some of its members. Some employees may seem interested only in financial factors, yet the statement leaves room for them to expand their vision of what they can derive from work.

An effective statement of purpose describes not only what the organization is but also what it wants to become in a way that sets high aspirations. By pointing toward a desired future, it opens an ongoing creative process. Peter Block (1987, p. 107) says the primary reason for creating what he calls a vision statement "is to reinforce the belief that all of us are engaged in the process of creating this organization." Those engaged in creating a purpose statement need to know their organization not only as it is but also in terms of where it wants to go.

Purpose Drives Structures and Systems

The purpose-driven organization distinguishes itself by moving well beyond a written statement. It communicates those words again and again in all sorts of written forms, but it does not stop there. The key to its being driven by purpose is in designing organizational structures and operating systems to continually reinforce that underlying purpose. It therefore establishes tracking systems to provide feedback on whether it is moving toward fulfillment of the purpose. Purpose becomes an everyday reality that continually raises effectiveness because it is supported by mechanisms that keep people's attention focused on it.

A purpose-driven organization asks, "What structure will best enable us to carry out our purpose?" The existing strengths, capabilities, and competitive competencies are major considerations in setting purpose initially. Too often the question is reversed, however, and the company asks, "What functions should we perform that fit our current structure and organization?" In a tough, turbulent environment, an organization must make structure serve the purpose or it will tend to become nonadaptive.

A mature organization designs controls and tracking systems such as budgets, performance evaluations, plans, policies and procedures, and short- and long-term objectives to maintain stability and predictability. These elaborate systems for controlling employees and reporting on their performance can become superfluous or even detrimental to effectiveness. As an organization progresses from Stage Three to Stage Four, these systems are altered so they clearly support action in alignment with its purpose. Because the Stage Four organization lets its members know what counts, it puts the most powerful management system into play; intrinsic control is exercised by people who are trusted to exercise their sense of responsibility in pursuing the organization's purpose.

The purpose-driven organization makes purpose a powerful force for driving performance. It uses purpose as the basis for its strategy, which then shapes long- and short-range plans. It also looks to purpose as it creates its tracking systems, which provide information on performance in terms of how well the organization is serving its purpose. It tailors pay and promotions to encourage workers to attain the results the purpose implies. Each individual then is influenced directly by his or her understanding of the purpose itself, the flow of activity driven by strategy and plans, and the information and rewards coming from the system. (See Figure 1.)

All organizations influence behavior through their tracking and reward systems—official and unofficial. Performance

Figure 1. How Purpose Creates Results.

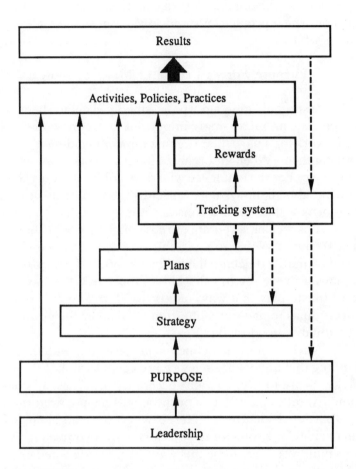

reports, financial compensation, recognition, promotions, new responsibilities, special assignments, access to more resources, and educational opportunities reward certain kinds of behavior. In the purpose-driven organization, reports and rewards are carefully tailored to ensure that people are serving the purpose.

As the organization uses purpose to shape its structure, job content, controls, and reward systems, these mechanisms make the purpose operational in the world of action. The purpose statement and these supporting structures and systems align members of an organization. However, they are not used in an attempt to set the organization in concrete. They become a platform on which people can stand so *they* can shape their organization's future.

Purpose Forces People to Make a Choice

An organization's purpose—the flywheel for behavior—will become an increasingly important factor in people's electing to work for a particular organization or deciding it is not the place for them. When the organization takes a stand, some people may leave. For the employee who does not fit, not only the purpose but also all the systems, structures, and practices that keep it in focus will serve as a constant reminder of any mismatch.

A particular corporate purpose might not appeal to everyone. It says, "We're going in this direction. We think it's the best direction." It defines the field and says, "Here are the types of plays we're going to call. This is the way we'll play. If you don't like to play that way, tell us; we'll trade you." It sets up a decision as to fit—not a question of whether the group or the individual is good or bad.

When a company defines its purpose, it is with the understanding that anyone from a vice president to an hourly worker might choose to say, "I can't accept these values. It's not the game I want to play." The purpose tells people what they can be a part of. It declares, "Here's what we're all about so you can decide if it's something you can commit yourself to. We're not saying you have to be this way. You decide whether or not you want to." When the organization's management defines what it will be, it is also defining what the organization is not—what opportunities it will pass up. It establishes a screening process in which people either find something meaningful or elect to leave. Managers or others who feel they could or would like to shape the organization differently, if given the chance, are especially likely to leave. They may hold a different view of what the business mission should be because of their personal skills or interests, or they may differ on the nonbusiness values the organization upholds.

Generally, management is inclined to operate on the assumption that everybody should be kept on board if it is at all economically feasible. Even when that is not the case, the lack of expressed purpose sends this message: "We'll keep everyone here. We'll try to make everyone happy. We'll be vague enough in our values, mission, and objectives so nobody gets upset and leaves." As a result, many people work far below their capacity to serve themselves and the company. The power of a purpose-driven organization comes from everyone in the organization understanding what the organization is all about. Employees realize they have elected to stay and continue to do so as they act in concert with the purpose. They are not simply present; they are committed to what is going on.

The Role of Leadership in Conveying Purpose

The purpose-driven organization's culture is different from the setting with which many workers have been accustomed. It offers neither the simple informality of a start-up company nor the high specialization and formality of a Stage Three company. Instead, it enables people to work in networking relationships rather than in strict hierarchical structures. The management role differs, too. While the start-up company is led by an entrepreneur; the growth company, by an administrator; and the mature company, by a person in a watchdog role; the purpose-driven organization is led by a visionary person who focuses most of his or her efforts on conveying the purpose to others.

The transition to Stage Four will not happen unless a top executive is committed to moving to this stage because purposeful action is important to him or her as an individual. Leadership is central to the creation of a purpose-driven organization. The purpose statement in the genuinely purpose-driven company is far more than a collection of words; it expresses ideas and ideals that a leader or leaders are determined to bring to life. Just as movement to Stage Two or Three is not inevitable, there is no reason to expect that all organizations will succeed in moving to Stage Four. The most likely reason for not doing so is the lack of a leader who can champion the establishment of the purpose and passionately drive the organization toward it.

Corporate purpose begins with personal purpose. A purpose statement created without personal commitment to it will result in a meaningless piece of paper—mere propaganda at best. Vision and strategy fail to come to life in many Stage Three companies because they are flooded with internal communications that seem to serve no overriding purpose. When someone attempts to introduce a purpose statement in such a company, employees are likely to see it as just another memo. A leader must have the determination and skill to step out and convince members of the organization that this represents something of far greater magnitude than a message from management. Ideally this person should be the chief executive. He should at least be someone near enough to the top to have a central role as champion and shape the systems needed to support the purpose.

This book is directed to the person who can benefit from suggestions for leveraging the purpose he or she already has into a corporate purpose. In the subsequent chapters, we will suggest the means of creating a purpose statement and the plans and tracking systems to support the stand it takes. We will also explain the role of leadership and show why it is inseparable from purposeful corporate action. You will see that the techniques we describe will be of little value to the person who expects to create a purpose-driven organization with techniques alone.

Chapter 2

ᗡᏕᏕᏕᏕᏕᏕᏕᏕᏕᏕᏕᏕᏕᏕᏕᏕᏕᏕᏕᏕᏕᏕ

How Purpose Provides Direction and Inspires Commitment

In the past, management could often allow its corporate ship to coast along in a direction dictated largely by history. It could create incremental improvements in organizational effectiveness by changing something "out there" through techniques that altered or controlled the behavior of others in the organization.

As one corporate ship after another enters the waters of rushing change and fierce competition, management needs a new means of directing activity and generating power. The effective organization of the future will not be created by tinkering with the status quo. The type and magnitude of change needed, so profoundly different from that in the experience of today's managers, must be founded on meaningful, lasting purpose. Even under calm conditions, people at any level can easily lose sight of their goal. Without a clear corporate purpose, they get caught up in short-term considerations or the search for quick fixes as they grasp for improvement. They do not reflect deeply on what they are trying to accomplish. They fail to look at what they are doing within a broad context.

Responses to Change

Without an overriding purpose to guide it, management may select the wrong responses to change or implement the right response in the wrong way. It may "cut the fat," for example, in response to the red flag of shrinking profits. Managers are likely to swing the budget axe at inventories, travel expenses, equipment purchases, and maintenance. Or they may make cost reductions by setting an across-the-board target such as "Cut 7 percent of all our costs." Without a careful evaluation of how each activity or category of expenditures contributes to the organization's fundamental purpose, programs that should be sustained or even beefed up may be sacrificed while those that should be eliminated are allowed to drain resources.

If reductions in the work force are made through general targets rather than careful, specific trimming, they can injure the organization and rob it of vital future capabilities. If programs that reduce the number of employees are not seen as part of a longer process, they leave behind a doubly weakened organization because they heighten the need to invest in the human resources that have been retained. The remaining employees are likely to feel insecure and are unlikely to bring to the job the creativity the company needs. They will concentrate on adhering to the rules rather than adapting to the changing environment. They are likely to become less and less adaptable unless they can attain some positive vision of the future and feel that they will be able to play a role in working toward it.

Another traditional response to pressure is the introduction of new technology into operating processes. Unfortunately, when managers face difficult times, they traditionally have been oriented toward investments that reduce costs rather than those that might create totally new corporate strengths such as a new manufacturing or distribution capability. If they view people primarily as a cost, they are likely to regard new technology merely as a trade-off for workers rather than a means of opening doors to innovation and greater revenue.

This view can lead managers into a dangerous trap. They may not realize that the acquisition of new technologies may require significant changes in operators' skills, corporate policies and procedures, and organizational relationships. If their organization is accustomed to standardization and incremental changes, it will be ill prepared to make effective use of new technology. Movement toward computer-integrated manufacturing (CIM), for example, has frequently highlighted organizational shortcomings. It throws out the traditional learning curve because the unknowns of design, production, marketing, and pricing can be worked out in advance by acquiring, processing, and analyzing all the relevant information with the help of a computer. CIM enables a manufacturer to make the first unit of a new product virtually as cheaply as the millionth one. A company can introduce product design changes practically overnight.

But consider the typical organization into which this capability might be brought—an organization in which it takes months to go through each department sequentially to conduct market research, perform product design, conduct engineering work, make purchasing plans, and work out marketing tactics. Each department has its own objectives to serve. Conflicts and delays result in failure to make the quick responses needed in the fast-changing marketplace.

The old ways of viewing employees and managing them do not fit many of the new technologies that depend on good people in good relationships, working in a creative environment. In a dramatic reversal from the earlier stages of industrial automation, successful implementation of some of the newer, computer-related technologies depends on the human factors of interpersonal skills and individual readiness to change. The people employing the new technology need not only new technical skills but also greater access to information and the opportunity to employ deeper levels of thinking. Management is challenged to merge people, machines, and information into a living network.

A company can buy the hardware and software to make overnight changes in product, but its employees may not be accustomed to simultaneous, interdepartmental decision making. They probably lack good relationships with other departments at their level because they have no overriding purpose to lift them above concerns for protecting their turf. Even upper-level managers are used to working independently and are proud of the particular departmental cultures in which they once worked. They engage in friendly and sometimes not-so-friendly interdepartmental rivalry.

Foundation for a Purpose-Driven Strategy

Neither old nor new management techniques will serve well unless they fit into the context of what the organization is and where it is going. Selecting one technique versus another can lead to chaos rather than greater effectiveness. With a corporate purpose serving as a foundation, however, the chances of the overall impact being favorable improve. Purpose provides a frame of reference for managers at the highest levels as they select techniques and programs, screen new business opportunities, and establish priorities for allocating the organization's resources. Once an organization knows what effects it intends to have on the environment, it can create a strategy to describe how to get there in terms of resource allocation.

Many companies create strategic plans and long-range plans to define success. They expect plans to set them on a course from which they will not waver, but in times of discontinuous change, setting a strategy has often proven irrelevant. The strategy has not anticipated the changing environment precisely enough, and seldom has it provided the mechanisms to generate the proper responses to unforeseen developments. No one has asked line managers who are accountable for results to provide valuable inputs at the beginning of planning periods or as events play out. Not only does their exclusion from the process result in less than optimum strategy but it also tends to limit their effectiveness in executing plans because they may not be committed to them. In a mature organization, goals and objectives may be regarded as ends in themselves; after an objective is attained, someone sets a new one in an endless, purposeless process. In the context of a purpose, however, goals and objectives are milestones against which people can measure change and its appropriateness toward a more distant state.

Truly strategic management differs significantly from long-range planning by staff specialists. It begins with top management taking a fresh look at the world, determining the organization's potential purpose in it, and developing the means for fulfilling that purpose. It involves looking inward and asking, ''What do we do well?'' It also requires looking outward and asking, "What is worth doing well?" Then management in effect asks all its members, "What must we do better or differently? What do we have to change to serve a special purpose?" Strategy brings purpose into the realm of action.

Stanley Davis (1984) says management's interest in such phrases as "back to basics" in recent years signals the corporate search for appropriate philosophical roots. And these roots are part of what he calls *guiding beliefs.* "Strategy proceeds from guiding beliefs," says Davis. "If strategy is a statement of what a company wants to accomplish, and organization is the vehicle for how the company will accomplish it, then guiding beliefs are the statements of why the company wants to accomplish the strategy" (1984, pp. 4–5).

Purpose also relates to another popular term in leadership literature—*vision:* a description of what the organization will look like when it is fulfilling its purpose. The closer an organization comes to enabling all members to understand the overall purpose and specific objectives that serve it, the better its chances of performing well. At all levels this vision guides people in their daily decisions and gives them reason to commit their best efforts toward serving something that has meaning to them.

Corporate purpose and strategy are not abstract ends in themselves. In very practical terms, they exist to produce results. Essentially, they integrate the behavior of people in groups. Actually, they integrate the behavior of people who are, at times, operating independently so that their cumulative effect is positive for the total organization as well as for the individual. Purpose and strategy therefore guide behavior. Although the notion of guiding behavior might suggest creating uniformity or robotlike adherence to a set of rules, by no means does the purpose-driven organization seek conformity. It needs diversity of ideas and flexibility in action to meet continually changing demands. Thousands of decisions and actions throughout the organization are brought to bear on a common commitment.

An organization driven by purpose nurtures divergent thinking, not groupthink, in order to produce the results it is determined to get. Clarity of purpose aligns people's efforts even while allowing for open disagreement. It creates a cohesion that can withstand diverse views on substantive issues. Because openness and a sense of responsibility for the total system focus on finding the best answer, people can argue about ideas without slipping into personality conflicts.

Management consultant Roger Harrison (1983) says there are two approaches to integrating organizations: "alignment and attunement." The first means "the voluntary 'joining up' of individual members of the organization, finding fulfillment in the larger purpose of the organization." He defines attunement as "the support of the individuals by one another and by the larger whole which comes about through a sense of mutual responsibility, caring, and love." Harrison cautions, "Neither alignment nor attunement is sufficient by itself. Organizations that are aligned but not attuned tend to be high-performing systems, which exploit their members. . . . Organizations that are attuned but not sufficiently aligned tend to enjoy and support one another but do not get much done" (1983, p. 220).

Setting strategy and implementing it, not the plans on paper, are what truly integrate an organization and get the right things done. Committed employees, not projections and controls, make an organization fast enough and flexible enough to maintain a competitive advantage. Popular business books such as *In Search of Excellence* by Thomas Peters and Robert Waterman and *Theory Z* by William Ouchi have given us grounds for optimism as well as specific examples of how companies have shaped themselves around sets of values. They have shown that the most successful strategies are essentially sets of values that guide everyone in the organization. These strategies can be wired in by the stated purpose and the tracking and rewards systems that influence behavior so people can live them rather than look them up in a book of strategies. (See Chapter Six for details.) Peter Drucker says, "Only a clear definition of the mission and purpose of the business makes possible clear and realistic business objectives. It is the foundation for priorities, strategies, plans, and work assignments. It is the starting point for the design of managerial jobs and, above all, for the design of managerial structures" (1973, p. 75).

Linking Mind and Muscle

The Frederick Taylor, scientific management concept of there being a single best way to do a job is acceptable for static situations but not for those that need fast and flexible responses. Companies now need to enable workers to continually reinvent the best way of doing their jobs. They have to enable people to make on-the-spot decisions for operating equipment, responding to customer inquiries, or detecting impending quality problems.

Much of management's concern for strategy is really a matter of tactics—a seldom-mentioned aspect of effective action. Tactics are becoming increasingly important in a fast-changing world where decision-making responsibility must be dispersed to more and more people. Purpose permits people to have work assignments that allow them to make good tactical decisions as they deal with the many unplanned events they engage in each day. The constancy of goals and values embodied in the corporate purpose allows for flexibility within a framework.

Strategy is not simply a grand scheme into which all the necessary thinking has been invested, and implementation is not blind action. If an organization is going to operate strategically, its members have to make judgments in the field as they observe and respond to changing situations. Management has mistakenly assumed that thought must be separate from and precede action, says Henry Mintzberg: "Strategies can *form* as well as be *formulated*. A realized strategy can emerge in response to an evolving situation, or it can be brought about deliberately, through a process of formulation" (1987, p. 68). He says some of the best strategies combine "deliberation and control with flexibility and organizational learning" (p. 70).

Kenichi Ohmae observes: "Many of the problems of Western corporations are related to execution rather than strategy. Separation of muscle from brain may well be a root cause of the vicious cycle of the decline of productivity and loss of international competitiveness in which U.S. industry seems to be caught" (1982, p. 226). He believes Western corporations suffer from too much strategic planning through which "smart" people tell "less gifted" people exactly what to do: "Detailed long-range planning coupled with tight control from the center is a remarkably effective way of killing creativity" (p. 224).

Source of Commitment

The effectiveness of strategy is, in large part, determined by the level of commitment of all the people who take part in its creation and implementation. If employees are going to implement plans and generate tactics, they must be committed to the organization at a level far beyond what managers have generally expected of them. Managers concerned about directing people to work harder and smarter toward meeting their objectives commonly ask, "How can I motivate my workers?" At the same time, however, workers ask, "What's the use? Why should I work hard?" Although they come from different directions, these questions point to the mutual need for purpose. Management wants people who are committed to the organization's goals, and people want meaning in their work.

In organizations without purpose, lower-echelon managers and nonmanagers often complain that they do not know what top management is up to or what it wants. They may feel that what they regard as the right thing to do is not what top management wants them to do. Young workers have confronted so many systems in their lives that they rebel against purposeless activity. If the purpose of a company as they perceive it does not meet their wants, they may go elsewhere or go into business for themselves. They tend to be more vocal about the purposes they seek to fulfill than are older workers, many of whom have been conditioned to be less concerned about their personal purpose at work.

However, a new employee may come to work almost as a blank slate. His perception is likely to be: "You're organized. Give me something to commit to, become part of, identify with. Give me a frame of reference." Such an employee is open to the organization's beliefs, goals, and boundaries. Even today, when companies are loosening their boundaries on people's behavior, employees expect to be provided a framework around important issues. This does not mean people have to be transformed. It means that they require a rationale or framework for ordering their plans and actions.

People want and need to understand the organization's purpose. They have questions, spoken and unspoken, about the purpose of the things their organization is doing, how their particular unit fits in, and what they themselves are expected to do. The organization that wants to capitalize on employees' potential for commitment therefore has to explain what it is trying to do—why it does what it does and why it is going to do things differently.

Employees can see that it is possible to get what they want and need from a purposeful organization—both financial and nonfinancial benefits. Purpose-driven organizations give people the promise of economic gain, opportunity for achievement, and good chances of being on a winning team that knows where it is going. The individual then is more likely to be able to say, "I can trust this company because it has made a statement, and all its actions reflect and support it." Purpose can help people find more excitement and satisfaction in their present jobs than in the traditional scramble up the corporate ladder. It can give them more self-esteem and feelings of significance than they get from salaries and titles.

John Sculley, Apple Computer's president, says, "Our people look for a clear vision, a set of values, and directions for the future as the forces that bind us together" (1987, p. 231). He notes that in some of the more progressive companies, people are looking "for personal growth, for a chance to make an important contribution. They want to clearly understand the vison and direction of the corporation, why it's in business, and what that means to our society and view of the world" (pp. 123–124). In these times when many people feel little, if any, loyalty to the company, Sculley asserts that "the first level of commitment accrues not to the company but to its sense of purpose" (p. 126).

The sense of purpose burns fiercely in some people. They express it clearly and openly. Others come to work in need of a purpose with which they can identify. Whether it is a deep philosophical inquiry ("What's the purpose of life?") or a more down-to-earth question ("Why am I doing this work?"), people constantly express or search for purpose. It is a basic human need that satisfies the search for self-identity and for unity in some larger self. "Commitment to something larger than our own success gives life meaning," observes Richard Leider (1985, p. 8). Individuals want to be involved in groups with purpose. They root for the hometown baseball or football team. They want to be part of something outside themselves. This applies to the work setting as well as to social interests. "Both within organizations and in our private lives, many of us hunger for purposes higher than mere career success and seek a nobler vision in which we can enroll," says Harrison (1983, p. 211).

Whether an organization has a stated purpose or not, people will attribute purposes to it, depending on where they are inside or outside the organization. An owner may view an organization as an opportunity to make a profit. One employee may see it simply as the source of a paycheck, while another sees it as a playing field on which to win personal victories. All too often, people perceive conflicting purposes. Here is typical pairing: the belief that certain persons own or manage the business to make money versus employees who have to fight for all the money they can get from these persons. That is why we reiterate: Purpose attends not only to the organization itself but also to *all* parties who have a stake in its success. "Shareholders are best served in the long-run when corporations attempt to satisfy the legitimate claims of all the parties that have a stake in their companies: consumers, employees, suppliers, dealers, special interest groups, host communities, government," says James O'Toole, management professor at the University of Southern California (1985, p. 42).

Harrison advises, "The mission should reflect the highest purpose of the organization—values people associate with what they consider to be 'good' not only for the organization, but for the world beyond the organization's boundaries" (1987, p. 18). Financial measures of the organization's performance are highly unlikely to be sufficient for maximum effectiveness because objectives such as earning 15 percent return on investment or improving shareholder equity 10 percent per year do not capture the spirit of employees—managers and nonmanagers alike. If workers see an organization's purpose as simply financial gain for top managers, workers and the organization will be at odds with one another. Workers who are strongly committed to a purpose that is not financial are most frustrated of all; they may resort to activities outside the job for satisfaction of personal purpose.

Purpose for Power and Flexibility

Although purpose-driven organizations are results oriented they attend to both corporate and individual interests. If an organization is overly concerned with results, then it may run roughshod over individuals. Harrison points out that "the achievement organization . . . may not have a heart. Employees and their needs are subordinate to the organization's mission and its needs" (1987, p. 12). In contrast, a carefully constructed purpose can enable an organization to unleash tremendous power—the power that comes from people's commitment. To tap into this source of energy, some managers are becoming more creative in the way they structure their organizations. They are convinced that they will find the means to innovation and competitiveness in the realm of such concepts as values and commitment. They see purpose as the important determinant of individual behavior that it is. They see the potential for far more organizational power through winning workers' commitment than by wrestling for their compliance.

When clearly stated and understood, purpose provides something even more important than direction. It releases in people the power of determination to reach that end. When individuals make a commitment to a corporate purpose and understand how they can contribute to it, they can call upon power beyond anything they may have employed before as they focus their energies, talents, and learning ability.

Harrison suggests one ingredient of this power: "When we establish and affirm an intention and create a vision of the end state, we 'program' our subconscious minds to selectively

perceive anything which could help us achieve our purposes.
Thus, although we may begin with no idea of how to achieve
our goal, we will begin to see the means we need through the
filter we have set up which will selectively bring to our attention events, people, and other resources which could be useful
to us'' (1983, p. 217). Willis Harman, scientist, futurist, and
president of the Institute of Noetic Sciences, says: ''Once the
vision is created and there is commitment to it, the factors and
forces to bring about its realization are already set in motion.
'Coincidences,' 'lucky breaks,' and 'following hunches' are likely
to play a part; actualization of the vision comes about in ways
that feel mysteriously like something more than planned steps
plus chance events'' (1988, p. 166).

Purpose is the keel that can give an organization stability—
not the stability of sitting at anchor in still waters but of being
able to travel at maximum speed with good maneuverability.
Purpose-driven people know that because the world constantly
changes, the way to fulfill purpose is through not rigidity but
appropriate innovation. People acting with a conscious purpose
act *upon* their environment rather than merely reacting to it.
They work to impose their will rather than wait to be acted upon
(Quinn, 1988).

However, change needs an end point. Individuals and
organizations cannot change effectively unless they know what
to change from, what to change to, and what not to change.
People need focus for their efforts—whether it be in maintaining stability or encouraging change. As management observer
Thomas Peters says, ''If there is no vision, or if the edges of
the vision are very fuzzy, you don't know what is 'risk in pursuit of the vision' as opposed to 'risk for risk's sake' '' (1987,
p. 522).

Purpose not only provides this vision of some future state
but also incorporates memory or the retention of what has been
working well. People need to know they are part of a winner
with the prospects of winning still more. They have much at
stake in what is already developed. They need to recognize what
has been established and must be maintained to serve the purpose. Vision therefore builds on the past, contributing to stability
in those areas where change is counterproductive.

This purpose overcomes a fundamental dilemma in planning strategy—what Mintzberg refers to as "the need to reconcile the forces for stability and for change—to focus efforts and gain operating efficiencies on the one hand, yet adapt and maintain currency with a changing external environment on the other" (1987, p. 73). He cautions: "To manage strategy . . . is not so much to promote change as to know when to do so" (p. 71).

When employees see purpose at work in the organization, they are more likely to be willing to change their behavior or their organizational relationships in order to fulfill that purpose. Generally, change does not come easily to individuals or organizations. Most of us resist it. We welcome an occasional change when we are "guaranteed" an immediate benefit. However, when we face a change, we are generally apprehensive, and when we have an opportunity to create a change, we do so reluctantly. When we are convinced that a particular change can serve a purpose to which we are deeply committed, we are more likely to act boldly.

Purpose enables people to shift their self-perceptions, allowing them to see new possibilities in themselves. For example, a technician may get frustrated when a customer interrupts her work, but if she were working toward a purpose that puts the customer first, she would see that she is performing her work at her best when she serves that customer. Dedication to purpose also helps employees shift their perceptions of their fellow workers. They are more inclined to look for the potential in others to furnish knowledge or resources that will help them on their journey. Commitment to purpose raises people above provincial interest and frees them from feeling that they have to protect their job or their department's turf. It also lifts them from the struggle to win credit for themselves or discredit others because purpose leads people to recognize their interdependence. It encourages teamwork.

Organizations that offer purpose and provide support for putting it to work make themselves far more effective than those that rely on outdated notions of controlling employees' behavior. The purpose-driven organization gives itself direction for its efforts, a meaningful basis for allocating resources, a newfound source of power, and a tactical flexibility for navigating the seas of change.

Chapter 3

಄಄಄಄಄಄಄಄಄಄಄಄಄಄಄಄಄಄಄಄಄಄಄಄಄಄಄಄಄಄಄

Establishing the Real Purpose of the Organization

We turn now to help the person who wants to create a purpose-driven organization. Good intentions are fine, but there are some hard realities to be addressed. This chapter deals with practical considerations for initiating the never-ending process of making an organization purposeful in all its plans and actions.

Getting started may not look like action at all because it is essentially a thinking and writing process. The first step in taking a business leader's vision from concept to reality is to define a corporate purpose and put it in writing so it becomes tangible. This statement of purpose clearly sets down business goals, values, and practices to guide all people in, and some outside, the organization. It expresses something deeper and more lasting than an awards banquet pep talk or the chairman's message in the annual report. It documents those things that are crucial for the organization's competitiveness over the long run. Even the best organizations are likely to be missing this solid foundation that enables people to say confidently, "We know where we are and where we are going."

A purpose statement differs from both the business mission statements that some companies have prepared and the credos that have long been popular. It is different because it brings together the best of each, answering people's questions about their economic *and* their noneconomic concerns. It contains a business mission that describes what business the organization is in or wants to be in. This description covers products, services, markets, customer needs, competitive advantages, and niches of the business. It articulates what the organization intends to do to satisfy needs in the marketplace. It provides performance measures so that employees can check their progress. These measures may be qualitative or quantitative (such as after-tax earnings, market share, customer satisfaction measures, revenue growth)—whatever the organization's management wants to use as the primary standards of its achievement. This portion of the statement meaningfully presents the business and what constitutes success.

The statement of purpose also contains a section expressing the values or beliefs that determine management's practices—how the organization should conduct its business. It describes in a broad manner the orientation toward the welfare and treatment of the organization's assets—technology, physical assets, financial assets, and people inside and outside the organization. The most important asset, which provides the energy for the organization to achieve its goals, and the one that should receive the most attention in the statement is people. This is where guidelines for behavior are set down for dealings among employees, customers, suppliers, and others.

Human values and practical business parameters may appear to be strange bedfellows. On the contrary, we believe that being in tune with the marketplace and the individual makes a wonderful partnership. It provides a coherent, integrated framework for people to understand the important whats, hows, and whys of the organization. Employees can work more effectively and efficiently when their financial needs and their other values are in balance.

Benefits of a Statement of Purpose

A well-developed purpose statement offers at least six potential benefits:

Direction. First, it provides direction and definition for the organization. A statement of purpose establishes what the organization wants to succeed in, what it does, and, in turn, what it does not do. As a result, it presents the parameters for resource allocation, strategic and annual planning, and acceptable opportunities for new or expanded business.

The chief executive officer of a large multinational firm says his company's purpose statement "helps us keep on track when we wrestle with product development proposals or acquisition opportunities. At one time, we were surprised to find that some new products we were flirting with did not fit the purpose statement that we had just recently developed. After some long discussions we realized that the smart thing to do was drop those new ideas that wouldn't fit or we would be spreading our resources too thin." This company's purpose statement reads, in part, "The company is in the business of developing, manufacturing, and marketing innovative equipment for the application of sealing coatings, adhesives, and other bonding agents under extreme pressure or temperatures."

Focus. A second benefit from a well-constructed purpose statement is the focus for activities that distinguish the organization from others. It tells people how and where to channel their efforts to sustain the company's strengths and competitive advantages. It also provides a framework for responding to changes in the marketplace or economy. When employees clearly understand the corporate focus, they know what to work at and, as competitive pressures increase, what to work at harder or smarter.

A multibillion-dollar construction firm experienced substantial economic and competitive pressures in the early eighties. Top management, having never articulated a purpose, failed to provide a new focus in those tough times. Many employees had been at the organization for years and felt they had been fairly treated and compensated. They were paralyzed, however, by the changing environment and felt that top management was losing control of the business. As a result, many key employees left.

Policy. A purpose statement offers a benefit that many proponents of individual freedom and creativity in organizations have ignored. It outlines policy. By that, we mean policy in a broad sense. Policy defines do's and don't's, that is, limits or boundaries for people associated with an organization. Statements of policy express the values of the organization, how the organization wants to be seen both internally and externally, and how it wants to attain its goals. These value statements are a stand the organization takes and a reference to what is acceptable and what is not. A statement of purpose therefore can simplify some decisions by prescribing what is "in" and what is "out." Consider, for example, these samples from three different organizations:

"We rely on the competence and integrity of each manager to ensure that good ideas are heard and used."

"Shareholders, customers, and employees trust that the company will make decisive judgments for the long term rather than short term goals or today's profit."

"Promote from within. . . . Keep facilities under 500 people."

Meaning. All of us want to be more than a number at work. We want our work to enhance our self-respect and satisfy our desire to achieve. In short, we want our work to provide meaning for us. A purpose statement provides meaning by defining something greater to relate to than the job itself. It offers a broader context in which to fit our daily work.

To be effective, a statement of purpose must be meaningful to the people associated with the organization. The determination of what is meaningful and potentially exciting should command the priority and attention of top management. A worker in a foundry explained *meaningfulness* well after he read the firm's new purpose statement: "I have worked here twenty-two years and always knew what I was doing. Now I know *why* I do it."

IBM's cornerstone of "customer service, excellence, and respect for the individual" is a classic example of how one organization has provided meaning and purposefulness to its employees for many years.

A midwestern designer and manufacturer of process control systems developed a purpose statement that conveys meaning and challenge. Its 2,000 employees are highly supportive of the company because it has taken a stand to create the opportunity for each employee to grow, participate, and be recognized as a contributing member. It states as an objective: "Create the opportunity for each of us to grow, participate, and be recognized as a contributing . . . associate." Another company offers the potential of fulfillment beyond a static job description by stating: "We shall strive to be a great place to work where every employee is trusted, has opportunity to grow and be promoted, is treated as an individual, and has the opportunity to be creative and rewarded for performance."

Challenge. A purpose statement challenges workers by establishing goals and measures of achievement. It tells what characterizes success and prescribes how to achieve or maintain success. People typically like a challenge. An effective statement of purpose tells them where to direct their energy to meet a meaningful challenge. One company describes its challenge this way: "To provide financial services in a manner that anticipates and fulfills our customer needs at the very highest level of quality and timeliness."

Passion. A powerful but difficult-to-quantify benefit of a purpose statement is increased enthusiasm, commitment, and pride in one's organization. People in organizations may respond to a purpose statement in ways that go well beyond passively accepting their part in the whole picture. The statement of purpose gives them goals, methods, and limits—everything they need to play the game and keep score. It then stimulates their desire to win. Victory means satisfaction for the individual as well as success for the organization. After publishing a purpose statement, the vice president of operations at a small company proud of its internal, two-way communication practices said, "It did not say anything we'd not said before to our employees many times. But it did give them in one statement our fundamentals. It not only reinforced and maybe clarified previous messages, it got them excited."

Wrong Assumptions About Purpose Statements

The executive who wants to reap the benefits of a purpose statement may rush into preparing one and then be disappointed to find it has little impact on the organization. The mistake is easy to understand because there are several common but wrong assumptions that may lead to the creation of an ineffective purpose statement:

"It is a statement of performance goals and desired results only." A purpose statement should go beyond the bottom line. It considers customers, employees, shareholders, the community, and society at large. If it reads like an accounting statement, it will not win people's commitment.

"It is a statement of culture or employee relations' imperatives only." The fact that excellent companies are driven by values has led many organizations to prepare culture or value statements on how people should be treated. But values or beliefs should not be stated in isolation. People also want to know how to orient their efforts to beat the competition and remain in business so the values can be perpetuated. When the officers of one large manufacturing company showed us their proposed purpose statement, we noted that while it was a heartwarming description of a humanistic climate or culture, it made no reference to profits. Surely, we said, employees are going to demand, ''All this sounds good, but tell us about the financial aspects of this business.''

"It is a wish list from top management." If a statement of purpose is not rooted in reality, then it is likely to be read as fiction. This leads employees to treat work as entertainment (at best) and put it aside with little consideration. This type of statement adds nothing to the purposefulness of the organization because it does not speak to most workers. It may even backfire because it signals that management is out of touch.

"It does not have to relate to the marketplace." The fundamental truth of every organization is that it must satisfy a need in the marketplace to survive. Therefore, every organization must look externally at its customers or whoever is a ''buyer'' or

"user" and understand the elements for success as they perceived them. An organization that does not conceive its purpose in relation to the marketplace risks creating the assumption that changes external to the organization do not occur, are
not important, or are totally predictable and manageable.

"Its preparation employs a bottoms-up approach." The essence
of top management's job is to set the purpose of the organization and to provide a vision. We have never talked to a top
manager who felt it was the job of employees at the lower levels
to establish a vision, mission, or purpose for the organization.
Although the participation of many people inside and outside
is useful for shaping the statement, this participation should
operate in the context of management leading the way.

"A purpose statement has to be general." There are two fatal
flaws in a too-general statement of purpose: (1) It lacks significance to people who would use it as a guide for their behavior,
and (2) it does not convey the company's strengths or competitive
advantages. A purpose statement should be specific to the organization and its particular environment.

"A purpose statement has to be specific." Just as it can be too
broad, a purpose statement can be too narrow, too limiting.
The world is dynamic. Technology, markets, regulations, and
competitors constantly change. The purpose statement should
not place a set of blinders on the organization.

An overly specific purpose statement creates another,
more subtle problem. It discourages innovation. In several firms,
we were surprised to hear people express reluctance to offer new
product and marketing ideas because, in their opinion, they did
not fit into the organization's scope of business. Pursuing the
matter, we found that top management would have considered
these ideas, but the business mission part of the statement was
so limiting that it left no room for interpretation and creativity.

"It can be prepared quickly." Managers of many organizations are notorious for their predisposition to seize upon a
popular management technique, decree its implementation, and
then either forget about it or watch as nothing happens. A purpose statement represents the core of the organization now and
for the future; it is fundamental, not an add-on or a program.

Developing a statement of purpose involves an exploration of the ideas and values of many persons inside and outside the organization. That requires time, effort, and energy. It may also include a discomforting reassessment of ideas or a clash of strongly held opinions by key individuals. It is not an exercise to be entered into lightly.

"It is a one-time effort and, if done right, will not have to be repeated." A purpose statement must have a lasting quality that comes from a careful business definition that will endure more than one or two years. The much respected objectives of Hewlett-Packard were initially published in 1957. Written after great thought and reflection on earlier growth and success, they still provide basic guideposts today. The Johnson & Johnson credo was composed by Robert W. Johnson in the 1940s and is credited as a major reason for the company's surviving the Tylenol crisis in 1982. The J. C. Penney idea was formulated in 1913 as the "cornerstone upon which the success of our company is based." Thomas Watson, the founder of IBM in the 1930s, hammered out the statement that many inside and outside IBM have regarded as that company's basis for success. Development of a purpose statement should take whatever steps are required to make its mark on the company over the long term.

Nevertheless, it is important to establish a process that allows for review and revision of the purpose statement at any time because the future has a way of fooling us and not unfolding according to assumptions. It is essential therefore that executives regularly review the purpose statement to determine its relevance. As conditions change, an organization must reexamine its business realities and its internal practices and compare them with what the statement asserts. One approach is to review the purpose statement as part of annual planning. In most instances, reaffirmation or minor editing of the statement will be the likely outcome, but assessment of its performance and potential on an ongoing basis is important. As one CEO describes his company's statement, "It is a living document, open to change and refinement."

"A good statement stands on its own; it doesn't need someone to go around selling it." Bringing an effective purpose statement

to life requires a champion who is absolutely convinced of its value, pursues it relentlessly, and wins other people's commitment to it. The champion leads not only in writing the statement but also in the continued effort to communicate it in word and action and incorporate its substance into all the company's policies, plans, and practices.

Are You Prepared to Write a Purpose Statement?

Unless you can answer yes to all of the following questions, you should weigh carefully whether developing a purpose statement is the proper thing to do at this time.

1. Are you confident that the benefits of a purpose statement justify the time and effort required?

2. Do you really believe you and your co-workers have something to say about the mission of your business in the future that will make a difference now?

3. Are you convinced that you have something to say about management practices and values that is important to the organization's success over the long term?

4. Can you afford to invest the time now to do the work necessary to prepare an effective purpose statement?

5. Are you willing to be objective in the examination of management practices and relationships?

6. Are you willing to solicit and use feedback from customers, competitors, and others to help management understand the needs it satisfies and how its performance is perceived?

7. As part of a top management group, are you willing to take a stand about your business and values and commit yourself to setting an example?

8. Is there a champion for the development of a purpose statement who is in a position to drive it?

Writing a Statement of Purpose

Anyone who has read statements covering business objectives or values of an organization knows that there are as many forms of these statements as there are organizations themselves. Indeed, one of the secrets of preparing an effective purpose statement is to make explicit the uniqueness and the distinct ambitions of the organization. This establishes an identity and image for all to see and for interested persons to give life to and to live up to.

Writing a purpose statement is a process that goes far beyond simply writing. From our observations of what has worked and not worked in a number of companies, we recommend a series of steps to be overseen by the chief executive for effectively developing a statement.

1. Check the top management team's commitment to taking a stand in defining the organization's current business, its vision of future business, and the management practices and values that should guide behavior.
2. Make a preliminary outline of the specific elements or contents of the purpose statement. Once you know the tentative contents, spell out the data collection methods you will use to determine current conditions and practices.
3. Collect and analyze information on the organization's practices and success factors in its relations to customers and other outside groups in the marketplace. Assess the company's competitive advantages and study how it develops its resources.
4. Envision the future, looking ahead five to ten years to develop a scenario about the business, markets, and management practices you want the company to be known for.
5. Construct the statement with an emphasis on success factors today and what they are likely to be in the future.
6. Test the statement's completeness and practicality with a few people before going public. This dress rehearsal should involve a cross section of people who have a stake in the use of the purpose statement. They will evaluate whether it is realistic, comprehensive, and likely to inspire commitment by those who will be affected by it.

The first step in preparing a purpose statement is to decide if management is convinced it is worth the investment to prepare an effective one. The top manager must answer this question because the statement itself, as well as the process to develop it, will be inextricably associated with him or her. That person's views and values will shape the statement and set the direction for the organization. Development of a purpose statement is not left to a group. The process is not aimed at developing the lowest common denominator. At some point, the leader has to say, ''Here is my vision, rough as it is.'' He or she then asks for help in filling in the gaps and determining how to complete it.

Top managers ask us, ''Why should we commit to the work of preparing a purpose statement?'' First, we remind them of the many potential benefits. Then we ask them, ''Do you have ideas about the present and future scope and direction of the business? Do you know how the organization should be managed to reach your goals?'' If the answer is yes, then we suggest they proceed. They have some of the makings for a purpose statement, and these things need to be expressed openly.

Developing a purpose statement takes time and energy that some people may feel is more appropriately spent on other matters. They may feel it inappropriate to ask the critical questions that must be answered and explore the major issues that will serve as a foundation for the statement. As we mentioned in our list of the wrong assumptions about purpose statements, failure to have a champion of purpose is a sure way to kill the chances for developing a useful purpose. Unless there is a strong commitment to the process of securing a purpose statement for the organization by someone in a key position to drive it, operational and routine interests will prevail. As with most intentions to change, it will be buried by the customary resistance to change and concern about losing turf unless there is a real commitment to creating it.

After spending nine months developing a purpose statement, a chairman of the board described the need for a deliberate, sincere commitment: ''It is like putting together a puzzle, only harder. You start by knowing you have to put the picture together. But you don't see all the pieces, know how many there are, or even where they can be found. Then we found that some of the pieces can change shape, depending on other pieces we picked up later. We are much better for doing it, but it was the most frustrating, head swiveling experience I've had."

The second step is to identify the elements or contents of the purpose statement. Earlier, we said that a purpose statement should contain a present and future description of the business and a set of guidelines to manage assets, with an emphasis on the role and value of people. Only with both these ingredients can people know what the organization is all about and consider what they can do individually or together to fulfill the purpose.

Because the purpose statement articulates areas important to the success of the organization, the obvious question to be answered is, "What factors are important to our current and long-term success?" The answer becomes a key part of the purpose statement. Several sets of people warrant an invitation to answer this question. First and foremost is the founder of the organization, if available. The question should also be posed to the current top executive, his or her staff, and previous leaders of the organization. Often overlooked, yet a rich source of company history and highlights, are long-service employees at any level; they have a good awareness of the organization's pulse. They usually can describe the flow of major events and important decisions that have led to the current circumstances better than others who have less tenure.

Specific elements of the purpose statement should be addressed to people outside the organization as well. Because success is usually operationalized as meeting a need in the marketplace at a price the prospective customer is willing to pay, the customer or user certainly has relevant experience and views regarding factors of success. Opinions from competitors about the organization's strengths and competitive advantages may offer ideas for the contents of the purpose statement. These opinions may be hard to obtain directly, but most companies we know have been able to do so through indirect means. Suppliers are another valuable source of information. Although many parties may offer ideas on the contents of a purpose statement, the top management team must make the final selection. It is their job to direct the organization and indicate the direction for effective performance and relationships inside and outside the organization.

The second step includes a description of how detailed information on each of the purpose statement's elements will be collected. Determining the important internal and external success factors invariably generates opinions on just what their current status is. Top management must determine the most effective way to get objective readings on each element. The people whose views were solicited earlier are not necessarily the best or only ones to comment on their current status or future role. For example, an organization's founders and long-service employees tend to see things as having been better in the past. They usually have a "good old days" orientation and a tendency to perceive present conditions more critically than others do. Of course, they may be right. But you should gather additional data to get a broader reading on the present and future.

Data collection can take several forms: interviews, group discussions, or questionnaires. One company used all these techniques. It interviewed key customers and top managers, held group discussions with long-service employees and department heads, and distributed a questionnaire to other employees. You need to decide who will conduct the survey—members of the organization or people outside it who may be more objective. Our experience indicates that both ways can work.

The third step starts with the collection of information regarding current practices of the organization and how it conducts its business. We recommend adopting an external perspective by asking, "How can we better understand and serve needs in the marketplace?" First, consider the customer. What needs is your organization meeting? This is not the same as listing the features of your product or service. Rather, you are identifying "why buys"—what the product or service gives your customers as they perceive it. Using the list of needs, separate customers into groups based on needs fulfilled. One customer group may be based on the breadth and availability of the product line, while another grouping of customers may be based on the need for reliability of service and spare parts.

Continue the interpretation of external information with an analysis of major competitors in each group of customer needs. To help develop a purpose statement, the question here is obvious:"What does each competitor offer that leads customers to buy from them rather than me?" Are competitors offering something that better meets customers' needs? Are they meeting needs your product or service does not satisfy?

After you profile customers' needs and competitors' strengths, you should next consider the key success factors for the business. These competitive advantages define what the organization does for its customers that satisfies their needs better than the competition does. They may be intrinsic to the product or service or extrinsic (such as price, channels of distribution, or company reputation).

Taking stock inside the organization follows logically after collecting external data. An internal survey will help determine the management practices and the major energy factors that drive the organization. *Energy factors,* a term Alan Frohman (1985) introduced, identifies the driving forces for members of the organization. They are the values and activities that harness employees' energy and interest to the organization's goals. This step is often an exciting and revealing exercise. Top management has stated what it considers to be important regarding the organization's practices and operations. The survey reveals how well these guiding principles match reality. The essential question to be answered in this step is, "In terms of management practices and relations, what really counts here?"

The discrepancies between prescriptions and actual practices may justify a review and reformulation of the values in the purpose statement—references to such concepts as trust, cooperation, teamwork, creativity, and individual freedom. The complexity of today's business challenges and the high degree of specialization in most organizations are heightening the need for trust and cooperation in day-to-day work. Creativity and freedom are important not only for individual satisfaction but also as essential energy factors for the innovation the company needs. We are surprised at the frequent absence of any reference to management practices or principles pertaining to assets other than employees. Management practices involving new or existing technology, as well as financial and physical assets, can make significant differences in organizational effectiveness.

It is essential to know the role these elements play or should play in the organization's success. Developers of purpose statements should think as broadly as possible in establishing what really counts in the organization. The survey will also reveal the inevitable inconsistencies between official statements and what top managers represent in their day-to-day behavior.

This survey will serve as a good test of the success factors generated earlier. If the organization is successful but those factors are rated low in importance, then something is missing that better explains current performance. One company that ranked its timely customer service as a key success factor discovered its rating from customers was not nearly as high as expected or desired. In a large retail chain where management agreed that making decisions at the lowest possible level was important to its success, a survey showed that most employees believed that decisions were being made at higher and higher levels. For this organization, the purpose statement was the first step toward reversing the trend.

Surveys on internal and external success factors may point out inconsistencies or conflicts between business goals and other factors that top management wants in the statement of purpose. For example, ''acquiring established companies in businesses selling to our current market'' may not be compatible with ''providing maximum opportunity for expressing entrepreneurial skills.'' The discrepancies the survey uncovers should be hammered out later in developing the purpose statement.

The fourth step, looking ahead ten years in order to identify what the organization wants to pursue to be successful, brings us to the popular concept of *vision*. This is not something that someone dreams up. It is, in part, the result of the hard work performed in steps one through three. Although the best vision may not be totally accurate, it prepares people to plan for and respond to future events in a coordinated and consistent manner. The vision does not eliminate the need for systematic planning. Rather, the work done in formulating a vision provides a framework and foundation for planning in its scenarios of how business conditions might change. This enables the organization to direct its plans more effectively.

The following questions are helpful in developing a vision of the external environment:

1. What trends and assumptions (political, regulatory, social, economic, techological) should you consider in the world around us?
2. What trends or changes do you expect in your industry or marketplace?
3. What trends or changes do you expect in your customers?
4. What trends or changes will affect your customer base? What might reduce or increase the need for your product or service?
5. What trends or changes do you expect in your competition? What do you expect your current competitors to do? Where might new competition come from?
6. What specific trends or changes threaten your current competitive advantages?
7. What opportunities to take greater advantage of current competitive advantages or strengths emerge from anticipated trends and changes?
8. What opportunities emerge from your vision that although not directly related to current strengths, merit further assessment?

Then management creates an internal vision to present a picture of what counts in management's beliefs and practices. These factors are subject to control by management to a much greater degree than those typically examined in the external vision. For example, managers can enhance the practice of teamwork by making available team-building programs. They can improve inventory management by investing in forecasting and information systems.

The internal vision is developed through careful response to these questions:

1. What trends and changes do you expect in your organiza-
    tion's financial and physical resources?
2. What changes or trends do you anticipate with regard to
    your work force in terms of number, ages, and skills?
3. What management practices and values do you want to be
    known for in ten years? Which must you sustain? Which
    must you develop?

The fifth step is the actual writing of the purpose statement. We have seen the top manager, the top management team,
a task force, and teams of internal specialists (each writing a
specific part) produce successful statements. External consultants
are often engaged at this step to help write the statement. Regardless of who writes the statement, there is one common ingredient
for success: The top management group thrashes out the final
purpose statement. Unless the statement appears to represent
those running the organization and something to which they are
committed, it is not likely to deliver potential benefits.

Writing the purpose statement means taking the original
proposal for the current business mission and management practices sections of the statement and facing the reality of how
customers, employees, and others see the organization. What
management wants to be known for in the future must be
matched and reconciled with others' visions of the future. The
final form of the purpose statement expresses a commitment
to how the organization will try to channel its business and assets.
It also indicates how top management will channel its own time
and energy.

Failure to set aside sufficient time to write the final statement is a common error. We have found that management groups
have different meeting styles. In some organizations, top management has spent several days away from daily interruptions to
draft the purpose statement. In one organization, managers met
once a week for four hours each time until they completed the
purpose statement. Follow whatever format fits management's
meeting style and allows enough time to do a quality job.

Then comes the logical question: "How do we know when
we are finished?" Essentially, the level of satisfaction and com-

mitment of the key participants determines the statement's completion. We suggest several test questions for members of the top management team:

1. Are you satisfied that you had your say and were listened to?
2. Do you think the group was as creative as it could be in discussing opportunities, strengths, weaknesses, and management practices?
3. Are you willing to now meet with your subordinates to present this purpose statement and tell them you are personally committed to it?
4. How confident are you that the mission and practices are realistic?

If the answers are affirmative, the statement is ready for the next stage. If any are negative, the management team needs to discuss what is missing.

The last step before managers formally unveil the purpose statement is a simple but important check of its realism and worth with a few people whose judgment is respected. Select people from inside and outside the organization to improve your odds of getting a balanced view. Ask them these questions:

1. Is the expression of our business mission clear and realistic?
2. Is the portion on managerial practices and values clear and realistic?
3. Does the purpose statement cover the things that are really important to our organization?

Extremely negative answers to any of the questions indicate more work may be needed. If there is widespread affirmation, it is time to start communicating the purpose statement to people who will use it. Unless it is communicated continuously and becomes the driving force for all the organization does, it is a collection of meaningless ideas on paper. Writing the statement will have been an interesting and somewhat useful exercise but not a step toward creating the purpose-driven organization.

~~~~~~

Chapter 4

Communicating Purpose Inside and Outside the Organization

"Why don't they know about it?" grumbles the president of a large company. Top managers spent a lot of time and effort last year preparing a purpose statement. They are proud of their purpose statement and feel it provides the right direction and challenge for the organization. The statement has been introduced in meetings at the company's six plants in conjunction with an announcement of the new annual plan. Employees have been invited to read the document, which is available in plant managers' offices. In his annual letter to employees, the president invited them again to become familiar with the purpose statement.

Much to the president's dismay, however, on his frequent trips through the factories, employees at all levels ask questions that indicate they are not familiar with the corporate purpose. When he asks them if they have read the purpose statement, they usually look puzzled. The purpose statement has not been communicated in ways that captured the employees' attention. Top management's excitement about the new game plan has been left in the coach's office rather than being put into action on the playing field.

Communicating the purpose statement is as important as constructing it if employees at all levels in all functions and external people associated with the organization are going to understand its direction and management practices. Unless the purpose is communicated effectively, it cannot become a driving force in corporate activity.

From our experience, we know that effective communication of a purpose statement depends on a few simple principles:

1. A clear presentation that captures the attention of the audience takes careful planning and the dedication of a person who champions the statement.
2. Multiple and periodic communication of the purpose statement improves the chances of its being understood.
3. Evaluation of the results of the communication effort provides a basis for improving and reinforcing it.
4. Beyond the dissemination of the statement, management must also support the purpose in all its actions and words and ensure that all procedures and structures within the organization support the purpose (as we describe in Chapters Five through Ten). Otherwise, communication will simply be pushing what people perceive as meaningless propaganda.

Most managers who have communicated their new purpose statements have told us that they wish they had put more time and effort into communication.

Here is a typical comment: "Having put so much work into something so important, we shortchanged our people and ourselves by not taking the steps necessary to make sure we got the message across."

Failure should not be surprising. Few organizations have any precedent in communicating this type of message. Top executives are not certain how to go about it or what results to expect. They may have no system in place to carry the message; sometimes they have to develop new means of communication. They must assign someone responsibility for developing the communications program. Top management may assume that managers down the line will inform their respective units of the organization; those managers may be waiting for someone to prepare a corporate communication program for them.

Management may also assume that the purpose statement will be greeted as good news, but some people are apt to be disappointed because it suggests shifts in resource allocation and business priorities. Some people will learn that their favorite products or programs are not part of the long-term thrust of the business. A purpose statement also puts management on the line by spelling out what ought to be. When employees, stockholders, customers, and others see the business mission and management practices as clearly stated guidelines, they may keep score on how well management performs.

Because communicating the corporate purpose is such a critical part of the evolution to purpose-driven organization, we next offer some down-to-earth tips and tools for those executives who are not communications experts. Eloquent statements of purpose and grand intentions for strategy and tactics are meaningless unless someone attends to the nuts and bolts of converting thoughts into action. Executives who want to avoid shortchanging themselves and their organizations know the importance of selecting specific audiences and media for communication.

Planning Communication

Communication of the purpose statement starts with top management establishing its objectives immediately after the purpose statement is drafted. Managers should ask, "What do we want our communication of the purpose statement to accomplish?" Their objectives should be as specific and concrete as possible. One approach is to establish short-, medium-, and long-range objectives. Then managers can evaluate the process's effectiveness in meeting these objectives.

Short-range objectives cover initial communication of the purpose statement. Here are some examples of short-range objectives:

1. Share the purpose statement with all employees and appropriate external people.
2. Generate excitement and interest in the organization's purpose.
3. Solicit ideas for fulfilling the purpose.
4. Communicate a direction and challenge in ways that meet individuals' various needs.

Medium-term objectives pertain to the year ahead and usually involve institutionalizing the purpose. You might use the following examples:

1. Improve the upward flow of ideas related to the purpose.
2. Increase the amount and quality of interdepartmental communication and coordination directed at achieving the purpose.
3. Increase customers' input to the product and market planning.
4. Improve communication with suppliers.

Long-term objectives, which extend beyond one year, focus on sustaining the commitment and establishing mechanisms for acquiring feedback that managers can use for revising the purpose statement as necessary. Consider the following suggestions:

1. Ensure the establishment of departmental plans and objectives that support the corporate purpose.
2. Increase participation in implementing the purpose statement.
3. Increase participation in the ongoing review of the purpose statement.

Shaping Your Message to Your Audiences

After establishing objectives for communication, management has to identify who should receive what information. We recommend dividing the audience into two broad categories—internal and external—and then segmenting each category further according to the information it needs and will use and its members' abilities to comprehend abstract and specific goals. Communication in one division, for example, may emphasize a narrower body of information than what corporate people are told. A communication about the statement of purpose for supervisors may supply less detail than one for top management.

Vary communication of the purpose statement to the degree that distinct needs and views among subgroups may affect how they understand or apply the purpose statement. As one executive told us: "Subgrouping forced us to consider what each group would think about and how they would react. It helped us be more purposeful in our communication."

The following criteria suggest ways to segment your audiences:

Internal

1. Geographical (local, national, foreign)
2. Unit (corporate, division, plant, department)
3. Level (top management, middle management)
4. Nonmanagement personnel (union, nonunion)
5. Compensation (eligible or ineligible for a bonus)

External

1. Sales and service (reps, distributors, service agencies)
2. Customers (key accounts, corporate accounts)
3. Suppliers (key vendors, potential vendors)
4. Financial community (stockholders, financial institutions)
5. Community at large (local government officials, schools, employment agencies)

Another factor that we find important in identifying audiences is the expected reaction to the communication. If a generally negative or critical response from a particular audience is likely, consider segregating it from the others. The communication plan for this audience should include a way to channel and answer complaints constructively.

Choosing a Communication Champion

The next phase of planning how to articulate the statement of purpose is to determine who will have overall responsibility for it, a timetable for activities, and the communication budget. We recommend assigning responsibility to one champion who has been heavily involved in preparing the purpose statement. This individual understands the corporate purpose, can explain the purpose statement's content, and is in a good position to ensure that the message is consistent from audience to audience. This champion of purpose relentlessly pursues the effective design and execution of communication; makes certain things happen such as having speakers or material available, arranging for a budget to cover expenses, and creating a schedule for the communication activities; and eliminates any erroneous assumptions about who is responsible. Because the purpose statement applies to the entire organization, one communication program framework is more effective than inventing frameworks for each organizational unit.

We have seen schedules and budgets vary from "quick and low" to "slow and extravagant." There are no magic formulas, but expressing the purpose statement is not business as usual and should not be treated as such. The potential benefits of effectively communicating a purpose statement justify careful thought to the schedule and budget in terms of the organization's size and the number of its locations and audiences. Furthermore, we cannot emphasize enough that the schedule and budget should allow for repeated communication of the purpose statement. We have compared the effects of highly polished, single-shot announcements to less-sophisticated communication involving multiple exposure. We are convinced that multiple and periodic communication of the purpose statement is essential. Cialdini (1984) cites studies from several social science fields that prove we tend to like things better as they become more familiar to us. Why? Thompson (1967) explains that repetition increases comprehension. After continued research he adds a second reason: "Secondly, increasing the number of contacts between the respondent and message results in added opportunities for shifts in beliefs" (Thompson, 1975, p. 440). The more often people read or listen to communications about the purpose statement, the more likely they are to develop interest in it. Repetition also provides more opportunities for people to find that their goals and beliefs are consistent with the purpose. They are then more likely to act to fulfill that purpose.

Selecting the Right Media

Choice of the appropriate communication media has a great deal to do with the purpose statement's impact on its intended audiences. For example, videotapes that clearly explain the purpose statement can have a strong positive impact on internal and external groups. Speakers and exhibits that cannot be easily assembled for extensive travel to multiple locations can appear in videotapes. While advances in technology have greatly expanded the range of alternatives for communication, they also present a trap. It is easy to become fascinated with high-tech gizmos and fail to accomplish your objectives.

Speakers often are central to communicating purpose. Success depends heavily on a speaker's credibility with a particular audience. The more credibility the speaker has with an audience, the greater the interest and acceptance of the purpose statement. In one organization, the CEO handled several of the initial presentations to employees and customers at nearby locations; the response was very positive. The local general manager or sales manager conducted meetings in locations remote from headquarters; although the responses were generally favorable, the impact was diminished by the lesser credibility of the spokespersons. People felt that if the purpose statement was important to the company, then someone involved in its preparation should present it. In this case, a videotape of the CEO might have been a better choice. However, being a member of the group that drafted the statement does not guarantee effectiveness for all audiences. For example, a top executive from finance or research and development who helped draw up the purpose statement may not be effective in front of factory or sales groups or with customers if he or she does not speak their language.

Determining which media to use begins with deciding whether the objective calls for one-way or two-way communication. If the objective is strictly one of disseminating or informing, then one-way communication devices are adequate. If the objective involves some form of discussion or action by the audience or data gathering, then two-way media are necessary. The number, size, and location of the audiences are your next considerations.

A task force of employees representing different parts of the organization probably can best sort through the enormous array of communication possibilities. The champion can collect their recommendations on how to most effectively communicate the purpose statement. In a similar manner, the champion can oversee using customer or user councils to develop an external communication program for the purpose statement. More and more companies are forming customer advisory councils to improve working relations. Because most council members are already interested in the organization's mission, it makes sense to share the purpose statement with them and solicit their suggestions for communicating it to others outside the organization.

Consider using the following communication tools to disseminate the statement.

Pamphlet or Booklet. You can distribute a document of two to two dozen pages containing the purpose statement. A pamphlet is only a one-way communication tool, however, and it tends to have a short life span. A longer booklet can explain the purpose statement, the reason for developing it, and its expected use. Most organizations rarely publish booklets, so this medium may underscore the purpose statement's importance. Booklets offer good, long-term reference value, but their look of permanence may discourage feedback.

Letter. A one-page announcement about the purpose statement can inform people of further communications to come. It may also be used as a follow-up after making more detailed presentations. A letter alone, however, cannot do justice to something so important and complex as delivering and explaining a purpose statement.

Bulletin Board. If employees read company bulletin boards, then they offer an inexpensive, quick means of announcing the purpose statement and describing the rest of the communication program. This traditional form of communication works best for brief messages. It is a reasonably good way to reach people within the company.

Display. Positioned in a lobby, a cafeteria, or a trade show, a display can present other media such as pamphlets, cards, pictures, and audiovisual equipment. Displays are fairly effective for introducing the purpose statement to external people who have an interest in the company. Inside a company, they are a reminder, at best, and may tend to fade into the woodwork.

Annual Report for Employees. This increasingly popular report usually presents the organization's financial and operational performance future prospects. Because the publication of such a report generally reflects a company's employee orientation, it is likely to be fairly well received. The report can reinforce the purpose statement by describing how the company has used the purpose statement during the past year or will use it in the coming year.

Annual Report for Shareholders. This is one of the best media for communicating the purpose statement to investors and other outsiders who want to learn about the company. The purpose statement can be explained in the president's letter at the beginning of the report or in a special section. Obviously, the business mission part of the statement will be of high interest to investors. These reports have an extremely long life.

House Organ. Newsletters or magazines for employees are often highly readable and, depending on content, may be taken home to share with the family. They are useful for reminding readers about the purpose statement, particularly if it is the basis for a regular series of articles. One large company used its newsletter effectively as a two-way communication device by providing a question-and-answer column about the purpose statement and its application. People who had helped prepare the purpose statement answered employees' questions.

Group Meeting. If planned properly, group meetings are one of the most productive communication vehicles. Participants have a chance to receive information about the purpose firsthand, ask questions, and get immediate answers. The purpose statement communicator can tailor the presentation to the audience both in the preparation and again in the meeting itself as he or she assesses the audience. The leader of the meeting also can solicit comments and collect information on reactions to the purpose statement. The effectiveness of meetings depends in part on the leader's presentation skills and ability to draw out people. Meetings do take time away from other work for the audience and involve preparation time for the leader, but they can be a highly valuable investment in future commitment and performance.

Meeting with Visual Aids. People retain far more when they see and hear something than when they only hear it. Visual aids can increase the amount of information conveyed in a purpose statement meeting. In addition, the audience is likely to infer a relationship between the importance of the subject matter and the quality of the visual aids. Some examples of visual aids follow:

> *Blackboard*—easy to prepare, but provides limited space and not portable
> *Flip charts*—easy to prepare, set up, and use
> *Transparencies*—relatively easy to prepare, portable, and easy to change
> *Movies and videotapes*—professional appearance if done properly, may be costly to prepare, not easy to change or resequence

A videotape is a relatively sophisticated vehicle that can combine the impact of audio and visual messages. It is useful for communication to geographically scattered audiences and for different audiences over a long period of time (such as for recurring orientations of new employees). Although videotape production is one of the more costly media, it does allow for the introduction of dramatic effects beyond someone simply speaking. Done well, a videotape can be highly informative and even entertaining. It is, however, a one-way communication tool.

Letter to Customers and Suppliers. Most customers and suppliers probably are not interested in attending meetings on a corporate purpose statement, but they do feel they have a stake in the organization. Letters can convey to them the highlights of a purpose statement. A single letter may suffice for all; several letters can be tailored for specific groups to explain how the purpose affects them.

Paycheck Stuffer. A brief note accompanying a paycheck is an attention getter. However, it is not a good place to present a purpose statement that deserves careful reading and thought. This device serves best for brief messages or reminders about the corporate purpose.

Plaque. A statement of purpose on a wall is highly visible to employees and visitors. Plaques can be displayed in many offices and areas throughout the organization. As a result, they can help maintain continuous awareness of the purpose statement.

Presentation Tips

Regardless of the communication vehicles you use, there are certain things you can do to enhance a presentation's effectiveness in promoting understanding and acceptance.

First, tailor the content and media to the audience. Communications that relate to or reflect some particular interests or characteristics of the audience are more influential on attitudes and opinions than are general communications.

Second, present advantages before disadvantages—give the good news first. When the desirable or positive aspects of a message are presented before the negative features, you are more likely to achieve acceptance or agreement.

Third, emphasize the positive aspects of achievement, not the negative of failure. Pointing out the benefits of following the purpose statement gets better results than does emphasizing the consequences of not following it. People want to be on a winning team.

And finally, draw conclusions for the audience. Facts do not speak for themselves. On complex matters such as corporate purpose you can generate more action by spelling out specific applications than by relying on the audience to make its own interpretations.

Measuring Results of Communication

So far, we have examined some of the work involved in effectively preparing communication of a purpose statement. Obviously, the most important indicator of the effort's effectiveness is the behavior and performance of people over time. Do they plan, act, and work together in ways consistent with the business mission and management practices described in the purpose statement? If actions and decisions conform to the framework of the purpose statement, then the message is getting across. If they do not, the purpose statement's messages were not understood or were not believed.

Measuring the effectiveness of communication is not the same as measuring the extent to which the corporate purpose is being served. (The latter depends on numerous other management actions discussed in subsequent chapters.) Here we are focusing on assessing the effectiveness of the communication process in order to determine how well people understand the information and know what to do with it. For instance, does the audience know how the organization wants to create a competitive advantage? Is the audience aware of the values for operating the business and working together? Does the audience know what to do to help the organization fulfill its purpose? The answers to these questions will indicate whether additional communication is necessary.

You can use a survey to determine the form and content of additional communication. Soliciting reactions to the communication of the purpose statement indicates that the organization is serious about the statement. It shows that top management wants everyone to understand the purpose and live by it. People believe their interests are being served when top management asks for their feedback and takes action in areas where they want improvement.

Some organizations have conducted surveys immediately after the initial presentation of the purpose statement; others have scheduled surveys as a separate event after the presentation. When to schedule a survey depends in part on the medium for the initial presentation and how the survey will be done. If, for example, the purpose statement is presented in written form and the survey is to consist of interviews or group discussion, then they will have to be separate events. If you use a paper-and-pencil survey, conducting it as a separate event improves the chances of maintaining confidentiality. But if management wants to use a group discussion to gauge effectiveness immediately and the audience is not easily assembled, the best time for the survey may be at the end of the purpose statement presentation. Group discussion of reactions to the purpose statement offers the benefit of having people together so they can hear other people's views and reactions. However, group dicussion does not allow confidentiality of response, and some people may feel inhibited by the size of the group. One organization had individual managers conduct the feedback sessions a day after the initial presentation by top management. This involved the lower-level managers early in communicating purpose, thereby emphasizing their role in implementing the statement.

A questionnaire gives everyone the opportunity to offer reactions and permits feedback to be confidential. On several occasions, organizations have distributed survey questionnaires at a meeting with instructions to complete them and return them at a later time. This approach minimizes lost work time and gives people more time to think about their answers. Unfortunately, we have observed low rates of response to this technique.

A group survey need not involve the entire audience. A representative cross section of the audience or audiences can provide reasonably accurate feedback on how well the purpose statement is understood. Individual interviews are another way to obtain feedback. Although they do provide for in-depth discussion, they can be very time consuming.

The effectiveness survey should cover these points:

1. How clear and understandable is the purpose statement?
2. Are the reasons for preparing and communicating a purpose statement clear?

3.   Are the ways the purpose statement can be fulfilled clear?
4.   What additional information do people need?

The champion of communicating the purpose statement uses the information from the survey to plan additional communication. To do otherwise suggests a significant lack of interest in people's commitment to fulfilling the purpose.

How Two Companies Delivered the Message

A midwestern metal fabricating company with three plants and 475 employees implemented its communication strategy to establish with insiders and outsiders the image of a strong and uniquely qualified company in its marketplace. Letters from the president to all employees, vendors, and suppliers introduced the purpose statement. Then the president conducted large meetings with employees to explain the reason for creating a purpose statement and what effects he expected from it. He also visited major customers and vendors over a six-month period to discuss the long-term direction of the company and to seek their reactions. Top managers in quarterly management meetings reported feedback from outsiders and employees, and then they shared those responses in meetings of lower-level workers so all employees knew what was happening. The purpose statement was published in a special section of the annual report and included in employee handbooks. A review of the purpose statement became the first major item on the agenda for top management's annual planning session.

A large insurance company with widely dispersed offices forged and communicated its purpose statement as a way to reaffirm the scope of its products and markets and the distinctive qualities (such as professional knowledge, dependability, and long-term customer relations) by which it expected to be successful. It targeted employees as the primary audience. The CEO introduced the purpose statement in a special meeting of all members of middle and upper management. During that meeting, he organized task groups to explore specific issues raised by the purpose statement. The task groups reported their findings at a subsequent meeting that was videotaped. After the tape was edited and enhanced with additional material about corporate history and plans, it was shown at each company location. Local managers followed a corporate outline and led discussions on the specific implications of the purpose statement for their operations. At this time, the employee newsletter initiated a series of articles explaining the main points of the business's mission.

Management's well-designed, clearly communicated purpose statement gets people ready for purposeful action. Once that process has begun, management's focus turns from expressing general intentions to establishing more specific guidelines for what the organization will do and how it will do it. Top management has laid the foundation for purposeful planning and roughed out guidelines for behavior that will benefit the individual and the organization. Its journey to creating a purpose-driven organization is well under way.

Chapter 5

Planning Strategies with a Purpose

A new management concept often becomes a buzzword. Enthusiasts may either use it excessively or misuse it in practice, so that the real substance is lost. They may seize upon a new idea so quickly that it does not have a chance to mature to its potential. This appears to have happened with "strategic planning." Launched by Igor Anssoff in the mid 1970s, its popularity skyrocketed. Yet there is reason to question how beneficial strategic planning has been. One analysis showed that of thirty-three strategic plans established in 1979, nineteen of them had failed by 1984 ("The New Breed of Strategic Planner," 1984). In the following years, Jack Welch moved General Electric away from its highly touted strategic planning process, and many companies dismantled their elaborate corporate planning staffs. Why?

In 1987, Henry Mintzberg wrote, "Today we hear a great deal about unrealized strategies, almost always in concert with the claim that implementation has failed. Management has been lax, controls have been loose, people haven't been committed. Excuses abound, but often these explanations prove too easy. So some people look beyond implementation to formulating" (1987, pp. 68–69).

We have seen many companies respond to disappointment with their plans by turning to more frequent planning. Instead of conducting annual reviews, they then begin to review plans more often. This has several harmful effects. It makes

managers focus on the activity—writing plans—rather than on
the desired results, it encourages rigid adherence to the plans
to reduce time spent in changing them or justifying them to top
management, and it forces managers to get so caught up in short-
term results that they fail to observe major, gradual shifts in
the marketplace. If you do not know where you are going, it
does little good to double your planning efforts.

Many organizations formulate their strategies in a knee-
jerk reaction to current events and later look back to gauge the
success of these strategies strictly on how well they matched
subsequent events. The test of strategy should not be how well
it stands up to external events. The real test is how well it enables
the organization to fulfill its purpose.

The driving force for strategy should be the corporate purpose. James O'Toole recognizes the importance of purpose as
a basis for strategy and plans from his study of successful,
vanguard organizations such as Motorola, Dayton-Hudson,
Levi-Strauss, and John Deere. He concludes: "Without a purpose, one cannot do long range planning. All one can do is tactical maneuvering designed to win the current round of the
game. . . . Because Vanguard executives know where they are
going, their planning tends to be anticipatory, structured, continuous and long term" (1985, p. 266).

The first step in planning therefore is to review the purpose statement. If the organization has not prepared one, then
its first step is the preparation of such a statement. (See Chapter
Three.) Some might argue that careful planning eliminates the
need for a purpose statement. Not so. The purpose captures
the essence of the organization—its memory as well as its vision and values; it serves as the foundation for planning. Purpose *establishes the reason for planning.* Without reference to purpose, planning may tend to extend what has been done in the
past rather than point toward a vision of what the future may
hold. Furthermore, without a statement of purpose, planners
are likely to neglect the values that determine how the organization conducts its business and thereby how members and external parties perceive it.

In this chapter, we will discuss three basic approaches to strategy and show how purpose can enhance the effectiveness of each of them. Some organizations set *opportunistic strategies* to make themselves highly adaptive to unanticipated changes outside or inside. The departure of a competitor from the market or a product development breakthrough is an example of opportunities for this type of strategy. This reactive approach can be highly effective in dealing with significant unexpected events. Planners who use it believe that rigid adherence to a plan does not always serve the corporate purpose best.

In a classic work on planning and control systems, Robert Anthony made a strong case for opportunistic planning.

> Since no one can foretell the future precisely . . . it follows that, in some respects, actual events will differ from the assumed events that the plans were designed to meet. Top management wants middle management to react to the events that actually occur, not to those that might have occurred had the real world been kind enough to conform to the planning assumptions. Therefore top management does not necessarily want operations to conform to plans.
>
> Furthermore, since people are not omniscient, their plans do not necessarily show the best course of action; they merely show what was thought of as best when the plan was made. Subsequently, someone may think of a way to improve on the plan; indeed it is quite likely that he will do so as the facts and alternatives become clearer. If he does, he should act accordingly. For this reason, also, top management does not necessarily want operations to conform to plans [Anthony, 1965, p. 29].

Effective opportunistic planning depends on meeting certain conditions:

- The organization has systems and methods to stay up to date on customers' needs, market trends, competitive actions, advances in technology, and product trends.
- The organization collects, evaluates, and communicates information from customers, the sales force, and suppliers.
- The organization makes decisions in a timely way; it neither overreacts nor moves too slowly.

In a purpose-driven organization, tracking systems constantly monitor whether the organization is taking appropriate actions to serve its purpose. These systems check the effect of the company's actions on the environment and, in turn, check the impact of environmental changes on its strategy. They thereby call attention to new opportunities so management can call for more appropriate actions than those stated or implied in the plans. The organization dedicated to purpose is not likely to stay locked into plans that prove less and less relevant as reality unfolds.

Most start-up organizations and many small ones without a formal planning system or written plans rely on setting *individual strategies*. Because start-up organizations have no history to serve as a reference, they depend on a particular individual for guidance. Their planning activity takes place in the head of the founder or top managers who may or may not put plans on paper.

Do entrepreneurs and small-business managers simply use their instincts to set strategy? Hardly. What we know about successful entrepreneurs indicates that they have a strong need to achieve—to meet standards they set for themselves. They are driven by a picture of what they can accomplish. This drive finds its outlet and possible fulfillment in start-up organizations. In other words, people start their own organizations with a keen sense of purpose. They already have a concept of the business, its opportunities, and ways to realize them. The purpose statement exists in their heads before they create their organizations.

Individuals who set strategies need more than a sense of purpose. They also need:

- Detailed knowledge of the products, markets, and competitors
- An understanding of the cost structure of the business
- Knowledge of the organization's key strengths and competitive advantages
- The ability to estimate, with reasonable accuracy, the costs and consequences of changes to the existing strategy

The personal purpose that leads an individual to establish his or her own organization often serves as the vision for others who join the organization. But as people and systems and procedures are added, the original purpose may become less and less visible. Increased complexity of internal operations may reach a level at which the organization can no longer rely totally on one individual's sense of purpose.

Setting *formal strategies* invariably happens in organizations as they grow and attempt to master more factors on the inside and the outside. The process tends to swing toward either a financial orientation or a marketplace orientation. Those who use a financial-based strategy generally approach planning as a financial exercise. They set strategy primarily by preparing forecasts and budgets that cover several years. Their planning usually deals with the gap between desired revenue or profits and what their projections indicate will occur. They then have to either lower their aspirations or consider a new course of action to close the gap.

Planning that is too internally focused ignores the market and views the organization only in financial terms. Consequently, it may cause planners to overlook relevant external issues. Furthermore, this narrow viewpoint may lead them to underemphasize the potential impact of external events and the impact the organization can have on its environment.

When financial-based strategies are aligned with a purpose statement, their effectiveness increases in two ways. First, the purpose provides an overriding, long-term view of what the organization wants to achieve in regard to financial considerations. Second, when a gap between aspirations and projections occurs, the purpose provides the reference point from which to assess opportunities to perform better.

Here are excerpts from several mission or purpose statements that provide explicit frameworks for financial-based strategies:

The Travelers Insurance Company's mission establishes two financial references—return on investment and commitment to financial strength.

The Travelers is a leading company in the insurance and financial services industry.

Our mission is to provide:

- Our customers with products of outstanding value characterized by quality service and effective use of technology
- Our shareholders with superior returns on their investment
- Our people with challenging opportunities for professional and personal development
- Our industry and the communities in which we do business with dedicated leadership

In pursuit of this mission, we will continually strive to maintain our commitment to innovation, integrity, and financial strength.

Dayton-Hudson Corporation, a major department store chain, goes to some lengths to state the importance of growth of earnings and return on investment. Anyone reading this statement gets a clear idea of the company's financial priorities and strategy:

Dayton-Hudson aims to be a premier investment. That means giving our shareholders a superior return on their investment.

To do that we strive for premier performance as measured against standards recognized by the financial community and as compared with our retail competitors.

One of the corporation's most important responsibilities is the objective measurement of performance.

For us, the two most important measures are Growth in Earnings and Return on Investment.

Because it tells the most about our performance, ROI is central to achieving our financial objectives. It helps us decide:

- Which capital projects to fund
- Which strategies to approve
- Which operating companies merit additional investment

ROI is to the financial side of our business what "value" is to the merchandising side.

Managing the Balance Sheet

At Dayton-Hudson, we believe you can't have a premier growth company without a strong and conservative capital structure.

We also believe you can't maintain either premier growth or a strong balance sheet without financial policies and objectives.

- We have strict guidelines for committing capital for expansion.
- We fund most of our growth internally.
- We pay regular dividends, and increase them annually.
- We use conservative financing methods.

Most of all, we aim to be explicit about how we manage the financial side of our business. We aim high. And we spell out clearly how we plan to get there.

External, or market-based, strategies have the reverse orientation of financial-based strategies. Those who use this approach treat planning primarily as an analysis of the market-place. Putting great weight on outside events and forces, management begins with a study of the market for each product or industry and gathers data on customers and competitors.

Next, it develops plans to position the products or services against the competition in specific markets. Product or market strategy then governs how resources are allocated. For example, new products may require additional research and development; new markets may require new promotion programs or distribution channels.

The weakness of this approach is that it underemphasizes the organization's operational and internal activities. It may not only disregard the capability of the organization to respond to the marketplace but it may also harm that capability. A market-based orientation may give the impression that the organization is run by the sales department and thereby undermine the cooperation necessary to execute the plans.

A purpose statement, by describing current and future business and customer needs that the organization endeavors to satisfy, provides the essential foundation for external-based planning. The organization's purpose gives a definition of the business; the strategy then defines how that business will be mastered. External-based strategy often raises issues and ideas concerning products, customers, and markets; the purpose statement can guide resolution of these matters. If strategies begin falling outside the frame of reference established by the purpose statement, management must either reconsider them or call into question the purpose itself.

The following examples illustrate how corporate statements can establish frameworks for considering marketplace strategies.

ITT Barton's business mission statement is specific about its products for the control and measurement of fluid properties. The statement presents a list of markets served and, notably, leaves the list open ended:

The Unit's mission is to serve industry and government with quality instruments used for the primary measurement analysis and local control of fluid flow, level, pressure, temperature, and fluid properties. This instrumentation includes flow meters, electronic readouts, indicators, recorders, switches, liquid level systems, analytical instruments such as titrators, integrators, controllers, transmitters, and various instruments for the measurement of fluid properties (density, viscosity, gravity) used for process variable sensing, data collection, control, and transmission. The Unit's mission includes fundamental "loopclosing" control and display devices when economically justified, but excludes broadline central control room instrumentation, systems design, and turnkey responsibility.

Markets served include instrumentation for oil and gas production, gas transportation, chemical and petrochemical processing, cryogenics, power generation, aerospace, government and marine, as well as other instrument and equipment manufacturers.

Perfection Corporation designs, manufactures, and markets engineered pipe products in the midwest. Its statement describes the current business and then lets us know the company is very interested in future business that uses its current expertise:

Our current business description is: Be a growing and profitable manufacturer of high quality products for the natural gas, appliance, plumbing and industrial supply industries, based primarily on the use of tubular products in conjunction with engineered components. We intend to be alert and to be prepared to enter into the manufacture of products for other industries and to provide service through contracted research and development projects to whomever can utilize our expertise.

Ohio Presbyterian Retirement Services succinctly describes its business and its specific market orientation:

Our mission is to provide older adults with caring and quality services toward the enhancement of physical, mental and spiritual well being consistent with the Christian Gospel.

Tapping the Energy Factors

Up to now we have been discussing the ways purpose statements can supply the frame of reference for all types of strategies: opportunistic, individual, and formal (financial based or market based). The distinctive characteristic of a purpose-driven organization's planning is that it takes its direction from purpose. Purpose not only helps formulate meaningful strategy but it also improves the prospects for effective implementation.

Once the strategic choices are made, the resultant strategy has to be carried out. This calls for gaining people's support, commitment, and energy. Some corporate statements reflect the vital importance of winning support for implementation and recognize that the quality of employees is the critical element in achieving success. Ford Motor Company's mission, values, and guiding principles statement, excerpted later, stresses this point: "Our people are the source of our strength. They provide our corporate intelligence and determine our reputation and vitality. Involvement and teamwork are our core human values."

Although a few persons set strategy, it has to be implemented at all levels of an organization. Therefore it must be communicated not only in terms that clearly describe the actions to be taken but also in terms that win commitment. The organization must tap the interest and energy of the people who will implement the strategy and plans. In pointing out that planners may put too little emphasis on the role of behavior in achieving objectives, Robert Hayes (1985) states that strategic advantage comes from changing company behavior. He says further that changing behavior is far more difficult than making structural changes.

Implementation of strategy often requires blazing new trails and trying new methods. Therefore in addition to objectives, data alternatives, and timetables, planners must also consider interests and values that will move people to action. Alan Frohman (1985) calls these "energy factors" because they indicate what ignites the interest and enthusiasm of the people in the organization. When plans trigger the energy factors they are therefore more likely to be supported and implemented successfully.

Unfortunately, none of the traditional planning processes facilitates getting people on board. Formal planning processes, especially, rely on quantifiable factors, numerical analysis, and rational thought. This forces planners to examine data carefully, cluster events and information into trends and patterns, construct rational arguments, set measurable goals, and articulate action programs. The analytical approach presumes that the world can be successfully addressed with a plan. Although we believe analysis and quantification are valuable ingredients for strategic decision making, we are convinced that plans do not cause purpose-driven action unless they clearly address the energy factors.

Alan Frohman (1985) says that implementation of strategy is directly affected by people's energy factors in four ways:

Their willingness to take risks
Their willingness to relinquish control
Their willingness to deviate from established practices
Their willingness to try something new

From our observations and those of Alan Frohman, we offer the following examples of these energy factors at work. Top management in a major aerospace manufacturer, looking to diversity, put together a task force to determine what new businesses the company should be considering. The task force examined a variety of possibilities, including transportation equipment, energy, computers, software, and medical systems. It spent two years evaluating the markets, costs, and other economics of each option. When the task force presented its findings to top management it suggested that the company move into photovoltaics in order to exploit technological capabilities that the company developed through its experience in defense contracting.

Top management elected, however, to move into a different field—solar power—even though the economics seemed less favorable. Their rationale for making this selection was

as follows: Many people in the organization were concerned
about its image as a defense contractor and wanted to move
into fields where it would be seen as a better corporate citizen.
In addition, many employees and shareholders would be willing to accept the higher risk of developing solar power business in order to shift sales efforts away from the federal government. Photovoltaics would continue the company's heavy
dependence on the federal government as its primary customer.
Attention to two energy factors determined the diversification
route.

The owner of a small company came to us with a simple
request to help him make a strategic acquisition. He wanted
to add a line of business that his employees would enthusiastically
support—something they could take pride in producing. He had
some financial objectives in mind, but he recognized the importance of the energy factors in making the new venture a
success.

The plans of a billion-dollar company in the automotive
aftermarket led it to make an "ideal" acquisition. The acquired
company brought a key technology that would revitalize the
products of its new owners, who already possessed strong marketing skills and customer awareness. This strategically motivated
acquisition looked like a stroke of genius. Three years later, however, the strengths and potential contribution of the acquired
company still had not been integrated into the parent company.
Tension was draining the energies of top-level management of
both companies. The strategy overlooked several important
energy factors needed to make it work. The acquiring company
was stable and conservative. It had experienced growth only
through internal development. Furthermore, it had handled
growth by adding to its original building so all employees could
be in one location. The acquired company was located in another
state. Its young, aggressive management differed markedly in
orientation and values. Both sides found it difficult to communicate and work together.

A fourth case: A multibillion-dollar processor of foods
identified, through its strategic planning, a gap in its product
line. It then developed a line of frozen foods, a category it had
not carried before. After a year of trying to sell the frozen foods,

the company realized far fewer sales than it had set as its objective, and it had a grumbling sales force on its hands. Entrance into the frozen foods business required that its salespeople relate to their customers in a new way. Although some parameters of quality and price are similar for all foods, the technical aspects of selling can differ significantly. Frozen foods have to be sold differently from other foods because they compete for freezer space in the stores. Furthermore, the sale of a new item might replace the sale of an item from the traditional lines that the salespeople are more accustomed to selling. In this case, the salespeople, who operated on commission, were used to emphasizing the foods they could sell easily and quickly—the items for which the company had an established reputation. Again, energy factors relevant to implementing the strategy had not been taken into account in formulating the strategy. They were left working against successful implementation of the new plans.

Still another example shows how the struggle for control can play a critical role in executing plans. A large producer of consumer goods took steps to compensate for a product that was maturing. It shifted its strategy from being technology driven to being driven more by its customers. Top management said the sales department would have more influence in formulating the organization's technical plans. Management thought this would result in greater market responsiveness, more products, and the development of products better designed to meet customers' needs. It developed ambitious goals in terms of greater market share and revenues. After several years had passed, however, the company had not met any of these goals.

Attempting to give the sales department greater influence raised the issue of control—a touchy energy factor. The organization had been driven by technology. It was dominated by R&D people, who called the shots. Although the new strategy called for increased influence by the sales organization, it was difficult for the technical people, who had been running their own show, to accept this intended shift. They were proud of their record and believed that they coould maintain their prime position even under the new strategy.

As these cases illustrate, plans may fail when energy factors are not considered. Here are signs of trouble:

People resist the plan.

Operating decisions establish priorities that do not match the plan.

The company misses opportunities in the marketplace.

People become frustrated and question the effectiveness of the plan.

A purpose statement can and should address energy factors in two ways. First, it can identify the important factors so they can influence formulations of strategy. Second, it can serve as a continual prompt to elicit discussion about tasks, control issues, and doing things differently that affect the motivation for implementing strategy.

In our work, we have come across a number of corporate statements that address the energy factors so important for winning support for implementation of plans. The following excerpts suggest the wide range of factors and ways of addressing them.

Rolm, a telephone equipment manufacturer specializing in office telephone systems (a unit of IBM's communications business), sees the energy factors related to having "a great place to work." This in turn depends heavily on challenging work and enhancing each employee's self-image. Note that employees' responsibilities are spelled out, too:

To earn a profit.

To grow.

To offer quality products and customer support.

To create a great place to work.

The company defines "great place to work" as meaning:

1. Work should be a challenging, stimulating and enjoyable experience.

2. The workplace should be pleasant.

3. ROLM should have an environment where every employee can enhance one's self-image through achievement, creativity and constructive feedback. Therefore, every employee should have:

1. Equal opportunity to grow and be promoted.
2. Treatment as an individual.
3. Personal privacy respected.
4. Encouragement and assistance to succeed.
5. Opportunity to be creative.
6. Evaluations based on job performance only.

Employee' responsibilities include:

1. Being honest.
2. Being helpful toward others to enhance teamwork.
3. Performing to the best of his or her abilities.
4. Helping to make ROLM a great place to work.
5. Understanding and supporting ROLM's goals.

Raychem Corporation, producer of insulation products, and Rolm have a comparable view of energy factors that win people's support and best effort. However, Raychem clearly places the responsibility upon managers to create conditions that engage these energy factors:

We believe that people work best in an atmosphere which is vigorous and stimulating rather than unnecessarily limiting. To provide this atmosphere, we encourage each employee to become involved with the job, to find better ways of doing it and to make his or her ideas heard.

We attempt to select managers who are involved and enthusiastic and who can spark enthusiasm in those with whom they work.

We encourage our managers to define and communicate important decisions, and to give each person the freedom to work within his or her own style toward the common goal.

We rely on the competence and integrity of each manager to ensure that good ideas are heard and used.

We maintain an open-door policy which protects the right of each individual to discuss his or her ideas or problems with anyone in the company.

We encourage outstanding performance and strive to recognize and reward it.

We attempt to provide a safe, pleasant working environment.

We insist that fairness and integrity permeate all decisions we make concerning our people, our products and our customers.

The interesting thing about Perfection Corporation's mission is the implied premise that people are motivated by activities that serve the customer. We have seen too few purpose statements that connect energy factors and service to customers as part of their corporate frame of reference:

Perfection believes in creating an atmosphere in which people working together:

- Care about what they do
- Utilize their own abilities to make right decisions
- Focus on customers and uncover innovative ways to service their product needs.
- Promptly respond to problems and customer's needs in a professional and concerned manner

---

Some statements go into less detail regarding values and energy factors. However, they provide worthwhile examples here because each defines a set of parameters for the way the company wants to operate. As such, each serves as a catalyst for discussions relating to formulating and winning support for implementation by people throughout the organization.

This brief excerpt from New York Life Insurance Company's statement says a lot. Notice that it describes the product and competitive advantages in the first sentence and how it wants to operate and tap the energy factors in the second:

We are a caring company, a leader in financial services, dedicated to providing our clients with value and financial security in the products we offer and quality and responsiveness in the services we provide. We are striving to be an aggressive team of enthusiastic professionals crusading to Be the Best.

Mars, Inc., a multibillion-dollar food company, in its statement of "five principles," is strikingly direct and business-like. Each point sounds like a commandment:

1. The consumer is our boss, quality is our work and value for money is our goal.
2. As individuals, we demand total responsibility from ourselves; as associates, we support the responsibilities of others.
3. A mutual benefit is a shared benefit; a shared benefit will endure.
4. We use resources to the full, waste nothing and do only what we can do best.
5. We need freedom to shape our future; we need profit to remain free.

The mission statement of *Industry Week* magazine balances business considerations and energy factors. It features the purpose of the organization in a broad context of the world economy:

1. INDUSTRY WEEK is a business publication written for management in industrial, financial, and industrial support service organizations. It strives to be "must" reading on issues that concern executive effectiveness at the personal, corporate, and societal levels and to inspire them to action.

Its editorial staff is dedicated to the well-being of its audience, their industries, and of the society which that audience serves. It supports a strong, balanced U.S. economy as part of a dynamic and growing world economy.

2. INDUSTRY WEEK is an advertising medium for those who sell goods and services used in its audience's businesses.

Its advertising opportunities are sold by persons dedicated to improving the effectiveness of their clients' marketing efforts.

3. INDUSTRY WEEK strives to be a business organization that serves as a model for promoting self-development and service to others, insisting on open communications and cooperation in Penton Publishing Co. and with support services in order to ensure the creation of the best possible value for the reader and the advertiser.

The members of this organization recognize the importance of continually improving revenues and efficiencies in order to maximize the value delivered to its readers and advertisers and the financial return to employees and shareholders.

The organization's members strive to maintain the highest integrity in their personal and professional lives, pursuing excellence, realizing self-worth on the job, and respecting one another.

Ford Motor Company's statement of mission, values, and guiding principles presents points of reference for more detailed planning. The business, marketplace strategy, and management approach are expressed in a straightforward style. This is an example of a purpose statement that can be an effective catalyst for discussions about plans:

Mission

Ford Motor Company is a worldwide leader in automotive and automotive-related products and services as well as in newer industries such as aerospace, communications, and financial services. Our mission is to improve continually our products and services to meet our customers' needs, allowing us to prosper as a business and to provide a reasonable return for our stockholders, the owners of our business.

Values

How we accomplish our mission is as important as the mission itself. Fundamental to success for the Company are these basic values:

People—Our people are the source of our strength. They provide our corporate intelligence and determine our reputation and vitality. Involvement and teamwork are our core human values.

Products—Our products are the end result of our efforts, and they should be the best in serving customers worldwide. As our products are viewed, so are we viewed.

Profits—Profits are the ultimate measure of how efficiently we provide customers with the best products for their needs. Profits are required to survive and grow.

Guiding Principles

Quality comes first—To achieve customer satisfaction, the quality of our products and services must be our number one priority.

Customers are the focus of everything we do—Our work must be done with our customers in mind, providing better products and services than our competition.

Continuous improvement is essential to our success—We must strive for excellence in everything we do: in our products, in their safety and value—and in our services, our human relations, our competitiveness, and our profitability.

Employee involvement is our way of life—We are a team. We must treat each other with trust and respect.

Dealers and suppliers are our partners—The Company must maintain mutually beneficial relationships with dealers, suppliers, and our other business associates.

Integrity is never compromised—The conduct of our Company worldwide must be pursued in a manner that is socially responsible and commands respect for its integrity and for its positive contributions to society. Our doors are open to men and women alike without discrimination and without regard to ethnic origin or personal beliefs.

A Cascade of Planning Follows Purpose

In most organizations, the planning process moves from strategy to long-term plans and then to annual or short-term plans and budgets. At each stage the purpose statement and higher-level plans provide the framework and define the parameters to be considered. This downward flow of guidance ensures that each level of planning addresses the business issues and energy factors important to the organization's future. At each successive step in planning, the purpose is translated into greater detail and meaning.

To illustrate how plans are derived from the purpose statement, let us consider the three examples in Table 2.

Table 2. The Relationship Between Purpose Statement and Planning.

Organization	Purpose	Strategy	Long-Term Plan	Short-Term Plan
A	Maintain technical leadership	Invest heavily in R&D	Hire 16 engineers	Hire 6
B	Expand into related markets	Add distribution channels	Add 20 representative firms	Identify 40 good candidates
C	Become low-cost supplier	Reduce manufacturing costs	Reduce inventory, modernize equipment	Improve inventory turns, scrap, and rework

The purpose statement for Organization A says it will remain the leader in developing laser welding technology applied to low-density objects. Therefore its strategy calls for a substantial increase in product development. That translates into a long-term plan to expand its engineering staff. The current annual plan works toward that goal by calling for the hiring of six experienced chemical engineers.

Following its purpose statement, the top management of Organization B made a strategic decision to enter a new market in the metal stamping and forging industries for its line of computer-controlled equipment for machining metals. The long-term plans reveal that this addition will require a new distribution channel to reach stamping and forging operations. In the sales department's long-term plan, this translates into the goal of adding twenty manufacturers' representative organizations to mount a new sales effort in the eastern United States. To meet this, the sales department plans to identify forty suitable candidates within the next year.

Organization C intends to become the nation's low-cost supplier of plastic-covered paper plates. Correspondingly, its strategy includes reducing manufacturing costs as an objective. The five-year plan calls for the introduction of modern, high-speed, reliable equipment and stringent inventory control. The manufacturing department's operating plan and budget aim for an increase in the number of inventory turns to 4.5 from 3.5, a 20 percent reduction in scrap and rework, and the hiring of an additional manufacturing process engineer in the next year.

Company C's manufacturing department will direct its reporting procedures toward monitoring data on inventory turns, sales and inventory levels, scrap, and rework. This step, tracking the progress toward fulfilling the purpose, is the subject of the next chapter.

Chapter 6

∿∿∿∿∿∿∿∿∿∿∿∿∿∿∿∿∿∿∿∿∿∿∿∿∿

Tracking and Assessing Results

An organization may have a picture of what it wants to achieve and plans for how it will get there. As we said in Chapter Five, effectiveness of that planning is determined by how well plans serve the purpose. People therefore need a tracking system that provides timely and accurate information that helps them gauge their effectiveness. Tracking enables members of the organization to know whether plans are being put into action and how well those actions are serving the corporate purpose.

Management literature exhorts leaders to construct a vision for their organizations, and some of them do an outstanding job of communicating a picture of the future for their followers. Of these, some support their vision with plans that address specific actions needed to turn the vision into reality. Unfortunately, too few of these leaders take the mandatory next steps to ensure that the actions are, in fact, put into practice and that they are producing the desired results. They fail to establish a tracking system to measure and report performance.

Vision is "in." It is symbolic of leadership in grand style. Measures and reports are not "in." They are regarded as tools for run-of-the-mill managers—not for leaders. Yet a purpose-driven leader's success depends on both setting the vision and tracking progress toward it. The visionary leader who ignores reporting is no more effective than the person who is excessively mired in financial and operating reports that have little relevance to the corporate purpose. Purpose without a tracking system is like a locomotive without wheels; it is powerful, but it does not go anywhere.

The top managers of one company initiated a formal review of its purpose, business objectives, and plans. They created a large notebook full of carefully developed plans and strategy statements. Two years later, a new vice president joined the executive group. During his first encounter with "the notebook," he realized that little had actually happened in the company to reflect these two-year-old plans. He also realized that the other vice presidents were satisfied with the company's performance and showed no concern about the fact that they were not meeting their long-term objectives.

This paradox existed because although top management had prepared plans and strategies, it continued to use the same measures of performance as in the past. Consequently it received no warnings that certain things were not getting done. Results, as reported by the traditional measures, were good, so management saw no reason to do anything differently. There were no measures in place to gauge progress or report the implementation of the long-term plans and strategies. The top management team had intended to alter the long-term direction of the company, but had not bothered to reroute the tracks. Things were getting done, but not the right things.

The new vice president pointed out the disparity between the bad news about performance relative to plans and the good news coming from the conventional reports and statements. His embarrassed colleagues agreed to fix the situation because they were genuinely interested in living up to the corporate purpose and fulfilling their strategy. They developed some new performance reporting procedures. In the following months, they were able to begin redirecting activities to implement the two-year-old plans.

Every company has a tracking system of some sort. Perhaps it is only the basic accounting system needed to keep the books and pay taxes. Even the most elaborate tracking system, however, may not reflect the organization's purpose and plans.

It may even run counter to them by providing data that draw attention to other considerations. Management has to ensure that its tracking systems are checking on the right things.

Tracking systems have to be tailored for each organization and for its different levels and units. Nevertheless, there are certain basic criteria to consider in designing any of them.

Just as purpose supplies the framework for planning, an organization's plans provide the framework for its tracking system. The tracking system should provide the information needed to report performance and identify midcourse corrections needed to fulfill the plans. This enables management to determine whether the organization is moving toward its goals and what adjustments, if any, are required. Management must ensure that it does not hold on to an established tracking system that does not serve the purpose. Such a tracking system will not help the organization follow its chosen course.

The tracking system should cover the full range of information needed to gauge performance against plans. We have found that people tend to skew their tracking systems toward information that is familiar, easy to generate, or easy to interpret. All too often, accounting-oriented planners concentrate on reports on internal activities and neglect to develop data about markets, customers, and competition—external factors.

Tracking systems may also be too narrow if they focus solely on financial measures. Although financial measures are the common denominator for most activities in organizations, they are certainly not the only ones or the best ones. Nonfinancial information may be harder to obtain and less precise than financial data, but it is often more relevant to the purpose. Nonfinancial information that some organizations have found important to track includes:

Trends in products' life cycles
Data on customers' satisfaction
Status of newly introduced products
Market share
Effectiveness of distribution channels
Reports of lost orders

Competitive actions and strategies
Developments in technology
Work-force demographics
Manpower plans
Status of implementation

A third key consideration in designing an effective tracking system is the degree of formality that will make the collection and reporting of information most effective. If all data are collected methodically, put on paper, and distributed on a fixed schedule without regard to urgency, the system suffers from too much formality. Furthermore, some information such as that involving changes in major customers' needs or competitors' strategies cannot be formalized.

As Arthur Toan, Jr., noted, ''There is really no quarrel for formality in its place. Excessive reliance on the formal collection of data can, however, prove to be a handicap, for much information—e.g. about markets, customers and products—is discovered by using informal methods which should not require rediscovery by formal techniques. Once obtained, there should be opportunity for it to reach the individuals who are in a position to use it.

''Excess reliance on formality can also harm the transmission of data to the user. It can slow up the process. It can also confuse the process by failing to provide for discussions that will highlight significant matters, clear up misunderstanding, and make sure that all parties see the situation in the same light'' (1968, p. 135).

Tracking systems may go to the other extreme and rely too much on informal data collection and evaluation. Purpose-driven action must be based on more than war stories about what is selling in the marketplace or the latest excuses for losing orders. Sizable amounts of data may be needed, and the data may have to be collected over a period of several years or longer by different people inside the organization. Management needs to strike a proper balance between formal and informal tracking to fully gauge its performance against purpose. The best systems can process insights and informal reports about critical events as well as statistics and quantifiable reports.

The tracking system should interpret information in a meaningful way. Raw data may be useless or even intimidating to some people. For the information to have meaning it must be interpreted in comparison to some benchmark or base such as the past, the plan, the present, or what the competition is doing. The strategy and objectives of the unit should suggest which bases of comparison are most appropriate.

Mark Potts and Peter Behr give an example of the importance of selecting the appropriate comparison base to Jack Welch, president of General Electric, "To Welch's management team, GE, like many companies, had become pre-occupied with imaginary planning targets that had little or no relationship to actual conditions. 'The thing that bothers me is that setting up a numerical target doesn't make it happen,' Welch says. 'It's better for us to look back over the last three years, clearly analyze how we performed against our competitive world,' he says. 'The degree to which we outperform industry will be the measure of our success. . . . If we under-perform industry, we will not have been successful in implementing our strategy'" (1987, p. 20).

The tracking system should measure individual performance against expectations. This is the individual's tangible link with the corporate purpose and plans. The tracking system in a purpose-driven organization continually reminds people that the purpose and plans are important. They pay attention to plan implementation when it is reflected in their performance measures. Information flowing through the tracking system can tell people their work is important by showing how it contributes to the plans and purpose of the organization. The information enables them to move the organization.

Accounting: The Backbone of Tracking Systems

Accounting information is the backbone for tracking that most managers understand and accept. The accounting system can provide much of the data for tracking but not all of it. Unfortunately, many top managers do not recognize this. They do not try to make accounting information reflect and support the implementation of the purpose and plans.

A tracking system should serve two key roles: enabling

managers to know how well implementation is proceeding and identifying new opportunities for serving the purpose. The primary role accounting systems play in most American companies, in contrast, is to satisfy external reporting requirements of investors and tax collectors. This does not mean, however, that the accounting system cannot provide information for both sets of activities.

Of course, accounting systems should be constructed to allow the organization to comply with external reporting requirements. But they also can be linked with purpose and plans to serve internal reporting needs. The company does have, after all, its own internal standards as established in its statement of purpose and plans. Overreliance on conventional accounting data as the sole ingredients for an internal tracking system has caused managers to overlook some of the essential activities that should occur in their organizations. "Managing the bottom line" means that the data coming from the conventional accounting system influence the way managers see their world. Consequently, they base decisions on data that may not be related to the purpose and plans. That is why managers tend to be preoccupied with short-term results and quick payback. This preoccupation is also reflected in the collection and reporting of certain cost and performance data that are not relevant to the organization's plans and goals. Thanks to the improvement in information processing technology, managers are flooded with still more accounting data that do little to help them stay on track.

We cannot condemn managers for being influenced by the system that determines how they will be rewarded, but we do urge them to take corrective action to improve the system. They should analyze what is coming from the present system that relates to purpose and plans. Then they need to determine what it is not providing and either extract that information from the accounting system or turn elsewhere to create new systems for collecting and analyzing data. They should regard the accounting system as a subset of the total tracking system they need.

In contrast to American practices, Japanese firms do not allow their external reporting requirements to dictate their internal tracking systems. Japanese firms have external reporting requirements, too, but they do not fall victim to allowing these procedures to limit their internal tracking practices: "Japanese companies tend to use their management control systems to support and reinforce their manufacturing strategies. A more direct link therefore exists between management accounting practices and corporate goals" (Hiromoto, 1988, p. 22). Overhead allocation is one way in which some Japanese firms drive their accounting practices to serve their plans. Some Japanese manufacturers' tracking systems do not try to pinpoint production costs precisely. Rather, they use an overhead allocation system that supports the company's long-term goals. Therefore, some companies base overhead allocation on direct labor when that supports plans to emphasize automation in the organization. Others base overhead on the number of parts in a product if they want to reduce the number of parts designed for new products (Hiromoto, 1988).

A second method by which Japanese companies may develop the data they need is through market-driven accounting practices such as using a sales price target that reflects the company's strategic plans and financial projections. They budget and track costs that are set to achieve a specific price required to ensure market success for them. A third method tracks costs in ways that relate to how efficiently a company must operate in order to fulfill market strategies.

There are many ways in which companies unintentionally allow their accounting information to run counter to achieving their purpose and plans. An organization's management may, for example, choose to buy a component or subassembly instead of making it. The purchased component may appear to cost less than the one produced internally because the accounting information has not been tied to implementation of the organization's plans and goals. As a result, the increased costs of purchasing, receiving, inspection, accounts payable, and other overhead functions are not brought to management's attention. These costs are not really being tracked and reported. Unless corporate plans allocate such an increase in overall costs, purchasing the component is not a good management decision.

If a company's plans call for a specific profit margin, some manager is likely to exert pressure to raise prices in order to create that margin. In turn, this raise may make the product less competitive and cause it to lose market share. In the next round of planning, management is likely to withhold resources because the accounting records show the product or business is not "making its numbers." This further weakens its competitive position.

Another major hazard posed by relying too heavily on accounting information is its tendency to generate short-term thinking. External reporting occurs on a short time cycle—a quarter or a year. Managers using it to track internal performance will tend to emphasize activities that show results in the short run, although strategy implementation usually extends longer than a quarter or a year. Such managers are not likely to take actions to implement plans if their performance tracking system runs on a different time frame.

Robert Hayes and William Abernathy (1980) have pointed out that severe competitive problems have resulted from overemphasizing the short term. They noted that, in the past, "American managers earned worldwide respect for their carefully planned yet aggressive action across three time frames: short term—using existing assets as efficiently as possible. Medium term—replacing labor and other scarce resources with capital equipment. Long term—developing new products and processes that open new markets or restructure old ones. The first of these time frames demands toughness, determination, and close attention to detail; the second, capital and the willingness to take sizable risks; and third, imagination and a certain amount of technological daring" (1980, p. 68).

Hayes and Abernathy made American managers aware that they had become adept at monitoring short-term performance and improving short-term efficiency, but perhaps were failing to take action for the medium and long term. This concentration on the immediate future has eroded U.S. competitiveness in the world marketplace: "Responsibility for this competitive listlessness belongs not just to a set of external conditions but also to the attitudes, preoccupations, and practices of American managers. By their preference for serving existing markets rather than creating new ones and by their devotion to

short-term returns and management by the numbers, many of
them have effectively forsworn long-term technological superior-
ity as a competitive weapon. In consequence they have abdicated
their strategic responsibilities'' (Hayes and Abernathy, 1980,
p. 70).

Tracking systems biased toward external reporting requirements are by their very nature geared to short-term results
that conflict with purpose. Purpose provides direction and
guidance for the long term. It often calls for development of
new products or new markets, technological advances, or other
innovative actions that detract from results measured by external reports. The tracking system needs to be expanded to provide the necessary measurements for long-term programs if the
purpose is to be fulfilled.

Accounting for the People Factor

A short-term financial orientation may encourage actions
contrary to the values and philosophy of the organization as expressed in its statement of purpose. As we illustrated in the
statements quoted in Chapter Five, some organizations state
emphatically the importance of their people making them competitive and successful. An organization may lose its competitive
advantage if the tracking system neglects to promote actions consistent with building sound employee relations, loyalties, and
teamwork.

Cost and accounting data for financial reporting will not
reveal deficiencies in nurturing a strong organization. To the
contrary, they will reflect cost-reduction efforts such as lay-
offs or canceling training as improvements earnings. These
gains are at the expense of the human organization. People
lose interest when they feel unfairly treated and exploited. They
no longer trust top management to carry out the purpose when
the tracking system contradicts it. Their willingness to put in
the extra effort diminishes—a cost that will not show up in an
accounting system.

We are not suggesting that cutting costs and reducing personnel are never appropriate in a purpose-driven organization.

We are simply pointing out that when they are not consistent with the purpose, they damage the organization. By the same token, managers who implement the purpose by building the value of employees through training, education, project assignments, and team building go unreported and unrecognized unless a purpose-driven tracking system is in place.

Top management, and especially the financial officers, must be deliberate in developing tracking procedures linked to the purpose and plans. Otherwise, financial staffs may be overwhelmed with new external reporting rules that require more work, reports, and systems. Top management that truly wants to balance short- and long-term needs in order to achieve its plans must restructure its accounting procedures to go beyond external reporting. Only by developing accounting practices to serve both internal and external requirements can an organization stay on track. Accounting information is too valuable to serve only external needs; it must enhance the internal working of the organization. It must not only keep score for tax collectors and the financial community but also help management make smart moves as it builds the organization's future.

Paychecks and Purpose

Managers should use tracking systems to report past performance and to influence future action by providing the information on which to base compensation and promotion. People may not be motivated by external rewards, but most of us recognize their significance as a scorecard. People will not commit themselves to purpose-driven work if they see that salaries and promotions are determined by some other measure than how well performance goals are being met. Rewards based on performance that supports the purpose will be icing on the cake for employees whose personal purpose is served more by the work they do than by added financial compensation.

If rewards systems are unrelated to purpose through the tracking systems, then people are unlikely to work toward the organization's objectives. More than one company whose objective is to increase profitability maintains a sales-reporting system that provides commissions on the basis of sales volume. Obviously, salespeople have little incentive to watch profit margins; they offer customers prices that will increase their volume. One company planned to be a leader in its market through aggressive development of new products. However, the bonus plan for its manufacturing division personnel was based strictly on efficiency. As a result, the management of the manufacturing division was reluctant to accept new products and insisted on many prototypes and test runs. This slowed the rate of introducing new products.

Compensation should reward people for performance that is related to the purpose and plans. A reward framework that is purpose oriented begins at the top of the organization. A compensation plan for top management that evolves from the purpose can avoid the common problems in executive compensation. Many bonus plans fail because companies allocate bonuses to executives on a discretionary basis; there is no relationship between serving the corporate purpose and the rewards. Others tie incentives to performance on factors that do not relate to the fundamental purpose of the organization.

Companies often use growth in earnings per share as their basis for executive bonuses even when that measure is, at best, only part of the corporate purpose. They wrongly assume that the stock market accurately reflects the degree to which a company is doing the right things right. They also ignore the fact that each organization has its own purpose and methods and must therefore reward performance accordingly. By simply accepting a single, universal standard, managers of these companies are taking the easy way out in designing executive compensation systems. They fail to support the corporate purpose because they have not linked incentives to the vision of how the organization will shape its unique future.

Chapter 7

∽∾∽∾∽∾∽∾∽∾∽∾∽∾∽∾∽∾∽∾∽∾∽∾∽∾∽∾∽∾∽∾∽∾∽∾∽

Supporting Purpose-Driven Innovation

A new product, a new production process, a new distribution system: The need for innovation in a particular area often dominates management's attention. This tends to obscure the organization's possible need for change and improvement in anything and everything it does. The more competitive the business climate, the more likely the organization needs a substantial number of changes.

"Most bold change is the result of a hundred thousand tiny changes that culminate in a bold product or procedure or structure," Thomas Peters (1987, p. 468) reminds us. "The dramatic symbol is usually just that, a symbol. The road to it is paved with a million experiments, a million false steps—and the wholehearted participation of everyone" (p. 468). Some Japanese companies have mastered the generation of incremental changes to become extremely successful in world markets even when they have not contributed a major breakthrough in technology. In fact, they have often been criticized for their ability to improve on the breakthrough ideas that emerge from other nations. They have created a virtually total involvement that fosters innovation in each and every task, which adds up to significant values in the marketplace.

Some U.S. companies are also intent on making change across the board—in marketing, purchasing, production, accounting, and product design. "Everybody improving everything" is their intent. They seek an infinite number of incremental changes as they encourage people to find innovative ways of doing their jobs and break down the barriers between jobs.

In recent years many companies have entered into long-term relationships with their vendors to capitalize on present and future capabilities to lower costs and improve quality. They have entered into alliances with other companies for joint marketing efforts, joint research and development, and shared production facilities. Some companies send employees to visit customers to learn how they can better meet customers' needs now and in the future. They also have employees visit suppliers or call in vendors' representatives to discuss quality or delivery problems. Companies then are relating to one another not just at the top but also at all levels. As they do so, the boundaries between them are growing less distinct.

This widespread quest for innovation at all levels is being assisted by the capabilities of modern information technology, which enable people to network regardless of rank, department, company, or physical location. For example, when the computerized monitoring systems on production equipment indicate that the quality of widgets being produced is beginning to fall to the minimal level of acceptability, this information allows for simultaneous responses in many quarters. If the problem is due to tool wear, the operator can request a change of tooling and, in the meantime, warn the department awaiting the parts that there will be a holdup. That department in turn can plan accordingly, perhaps suggesting the optimum time for the tool change. If the problem is due to faulty material, then the discoverer of the problem communicates with people in the earlier stages of the production process—even to outside vendors so they can make corrections immediately.

The more a company manages information effectively, the more it needs to allow people to relate to one another informally and quickly. Informality and networking are replacing the old concepts of hierarchy and control as they improve the speed of decision making and flexibility in action. Communication of information on inventory levels, technical specifications, prices of materials, sales projections, customer profiles, and customer complaints is quick and direct. No time is wasted passing the word sequentially through layers of management until it reaches a person authorized to make a decision and then pass the word down to others to take corrective action. New technology is demanding as well as permitting nonsequential decision making.

The need for dispersed decision making and innovation runs headlong into the rigidities of a Stage Three organization. Recall from Chapter One that while the Stage One company is the embodiment of change as it brings a product or service to the market for the first time and the Stage Two, or growth, company seeks major innovation in both its products and its own organizational structure, the Stage Three company strives primarily to protect what it has.

Innovation by a Chosen Few

There are two schools of thought regarding innovation and improvement in the Stage Three company. One relies on major breakthroughs coming from a few people in an otherwise stable environment. The other prefers to create an open environment in which anyone can innovate; it depends on incremental changes in all quarters and allows for breakthroughs as well.

The first approach to innovation is based on the assumption that innovation can or should come only from a small percentage of people in any organization. This assumption leads to the belief that these few must be encouraged and enabled to come up with a breakthrough development that will lift the stagnant organization to new heights. The mature organization therefore tends to restrict attention and resources for innovation to a chosen few—the R&D department, for example, or a specially designated individual who plays Caesar, commanding every aspect of a special project. It may allow or even encourage a "skunk works" operation that segregates itself from the main organization, breaking all the rules and taking isolated risks to come up with a breakthrough innovation.

A great deal of popular business literature has advocated the introduction of entrepreneurs or "intrapreneurs" into mature organizations. Unfortunately, these organizations operate with orderly, sequential procedures that generally do not encourage or support creativity. Calling for the injection of entrepreneurs here and there asks managers to drive their organizations with one foot on the brakes and the other on the gas pedal.

Research on entrepreneurs indicates they are marked by a need for achievement, a need to see something they create, and a need to be masters of their own destiny. They do not like structure or control and do not work well with others. They tend to be creative and persistent. Entrepreneurs clash in a number of ways with factors that make a mature organization work:

- Entrepreneurs seek to be autonomous and do something different, but mature organizations have reporting systems and controls geared to minimizing deviation.
- They have a high tolerance for uncertainty, but mature organizations try to promote efficient processing of information and decisions by reducing uncertainty and ambiguity.
- Innovators tend to be independent and unstructured and do not value conformity; mature organizations breed interdependence and coordination through structures and specialization.
- Entrepreneurs see their success as primarily a function of their own personal energy and efforts. They seek conditions that offer individual freedom, but mainstream managers see their effectiveness as a result of their ability to work with and influence others.
- While entrepreneurs look to express their own ideas and their individuality, mature organizations work to ensure consistent treatment of people through policies and procedures.

In other words, entrepreneurs do not exhibit behaviors that fit a mature organization. The conditions an entrepreneur requires—autonomy, responsibility, and an absence of structure and controls—are the antithesis of mature organizations. Conflict between the entrepreneur and the conventions of the Stage Three organization is inevitable and robs both of opportunities to perform the functions for which they were intended. Even when top management deliberately injects an entrepreneur

into the organization and is willing to tolerate exceptional behavior, the entrepreneur clashes with peers and others in the
organization who see him as an added buden in meeting their
objectives and as someone receiving unfair rewards.

An entrepreneur is like a foreign object introduced into
a body. The body's immune system will try to reject it in order
to defend the existing functions. The challenge facing most companies will be met not by the introduction of a foreign object
but by reconditioning the "body" to meet changing conditions.
Reliance on entrepreneurism in one or even several selected
areas does not address the need for innovation throughout the
organization. Mature organizations need more than a few individuals who buck the system; they need an entrepreneurial
environment for everyone that allows for smooth, fast shifts in
resource deployment.

Despite any of these efforts to inject innovation, the Stage
Three organization still has a relatively low propensity to risk
as compared with Stage One companies that are all-out innovators and Stage Two companies that are likely to be moderately
open to risk. In Stage Three organizations, people are expected
to prevent damage to the carefully constructed organization.
Many would-be innovators bear scars of failure because risks
that do not work out are dealt with in ways that discourage future
failure and therefore future risk taking.

The aversion to risk breeds a general reluctance to change.
When top management does try to implement a change in operating procedures or marketing strategy, for example, it meets
heavy internal resistance. It may overlook the fact that it is making incongruous demands on an organization designed for
stability. Management wants people to do new things, while
their experience and the company's tracking and compensation
systems support the old. From corporate headquarters come
directives for establishing new product lines or new means of
distribution that conflict with the current reporting procedures,
control systems, responsibilities, and compensation programs.
These directives upset the goals and priorities already in place.
Managers down the line who have to implement the changes
are inclined to serve the traditional expectations of them and

to wonder how to meet the new emphases at the same time. They see no purpose for all this confusion.

Innovation Anywhere and Everywhere

In regard to change in mature companies, the other school of thought, which is gaining popularity, holds that innovation is needed everywhere in the organization and can come from virtually anywhere inside or outside. It sees that relying on one Caesar to manage change in one area may insulate management from the truth. That person has a vested interest in covering mistakes or refusing to admit them. A more open system would allow the good and the bad to surface, permitting decisions to be based on merit. This school recognizes that while a few individuals can successfully bring innovation to large organizations, they are unlikely to do the entire innovation job most organizations need.

Students of this school regard new ideas as wildflowers. They know you do not plant seeds for wildflowers; you find them by searching in many places. They concentrate on preparing the conditions for wildflowers to grow as they push for incremental change everywhere. They fit well into the purpose-driven organization that strives to excel in everything it does to add value for everyone with an interest in it. The purpose-driven organization is designed to allow as many people as possible to take risks.

More and more companies are seeking ways to nurture organizational change that permits innovation to constantly bubble up from people eager to initiate and implement new ideas. At an automotive components plant, with an open system of employee involvement in which objectives and information are widely shared, incremental innovation has resulted in dramatically improved delivery performance and much higher quality levels. "We're not trying for the home run; we want continuous improvement," the plant manager there says (Pascarella, DiBianca, and Gioja, 1988, p. 50).

"It's not sufficient for our employees merely to list problems or spot opportunities," says this manager. Employees must be able to decide and act. "We have over 4,000 employees here. If everyone submitted 3 ideas, I'd be faced with 12,000 decisions." No manager or team of managers can have all the answers for all the possible questions that stand between the status quo and improvement. Additionally, they cannot make all the necessary decisions fast enough for optimum performance. The purpose-driven leader feels no need to conceive all the new ideas; that is not her job. Her role is to provide the mechanisms for stimulating, refining, approving, and implementing other people's ideas.

Most of us tend to think of creativity in terms of artists and writers or perhaps great scientists, but people express creativity in the many tasks they perform in humdrum daily activities. The truck driver who figures out the shortest route between stops, the salesclerk who can find just the right substitute for an unavailable item the customer wants, and the machinist who knows how to press his equipment beyond the engineer's definition of its capacity are displaying creativity without ceremony.

We tend to think of creativity in terms of generating something from nothing. But to a large degree, creativity is simply a matter of elaborating on the present, of putting old things together in new ways, or taking away from the present to create something simpler or better. This is the stuff of incremental improvement, and massive doses of it can make a company far more effective than any one-shot attempts at innovation. We may not be inclined to assume that all people are creative, but there are thousands of cases from the business world that should convince us that anyone is capable of being creative.

Increasingly, organizations will be built on the premise that anyone may have the capacity to innovate—that corporate change does not have to begin and end at the top. This thinking is supported by studies showing that creativity and innovation depend on individuals' perception of how creative they are and of the amount of freedom they believe they have to innovate. More and more managers are learning that every successful organization depends on people who are committed to making it work: the salesman who is determined to deliver value to his customer, the production line worker who produces only

what she can take pride in, or the manager who proves to
doubters that there is a niche for her product. These managers
have seen that in practically any company there are unofficial
champions of a particular technology or product, underground
pushers of new marketing techniques, or inventors of new organizational styles. Such people strengthen their organizations
because they go beyond the routine. They step outside their job
descriptions because they expect more from themselves. Top
management is challenged then to make such exceptions the
norm and to coordinate them toward some common purpose.

Preparing for Creative Action

The need to have many members of the organization
engaged in nonsequential decision making means workers at
all levels are becoming decision makers. This change has dramatically raised the need for a frame of reference—an overarching purpose—for making decisions. People need an established
set of values and sense of direction in order to integrate their
innovative efforts into a pattern that is meaningful to the organization. The purpose-driven organization provides this framework so people know what is worth changing and what sort of
innovations are appropriate.

Obviously, the organization that can combine the home-
run innovation with constant, widespread, incremental improvement is the ideal. Even a major innovation needs support from
an innovative organization if it is to flourish. Otherwise the innovation will die in implementation and perhaps take root in
another organization that can and wants to capitalize on it.

Too often, creativity is thought of only in terms of generating ideas. Managers frequently complain that their subordinates ''don't have any good ideas.'' They overlook the other
parts of innovation—the preparation and follow-up. Creative
people need to know the situation. They need to know what
ideas are relevant—where innovation is needed and where it
is not wanted. They need a vision of the future. They need to
see the gap between that vision and the present. And they need
to trust the organization and feel that it trusts them. When an

idea is ready for implementation, people need authority, resources, and feedback on performance. When it is not ready, they need to know why not.

Widespread innovation and nonsequential decision making are possible only when people feel responsible for offering ideas and when they are willing and able to make decisions about implementation. This requires management to shift from notions of wanting to control people to allowing them to exercise their creativity. A fundamental premise in the purpose-driven organization is that responsible action will come out of each individual's sense of purpose.

Innovation can best be managed by dealing with what comes before and after the idea-generation step. This means changing what traditionally goes on in the workplace; it does not mean changing people. It means changing the environment so that it is open to ideas that people want to deliver. Several factors contribute significantly to such an environment. They are traits of an organization in which people understand its purpose.

Knowing What Counts. As we noted earlier, people need to know what constitutes appropriate innovation. This information is framed in the purpose statement, in the supporting tracking and reward systems, and through management practices. One of the principal earmarks of a purpose-driven organization is its identification of areas in which innovation is important (and areas where it is not) and its translation of that information in terms of the individual's and unit's purpose.

Being at a crossroads or in a crisis may help management see what is important; people from the top to the bottom of the organization see what is happening. One company that needed several new products to fill out its product line was losing ground in the marketplace. Management committed itself to simultaneously developing related and not-so-related products in an "impossibly" short time. When all the affected departments heard the facts, witnessed management's commitment, and learned that the old rules of hierarchy were being abandoned, they responded with a surge of new products because they changed

their operating procedures and the way they related to one
another. People who had been "sitting" on better ways of doing things and ideas for new components came forth with a bar-
rage of suggestions. The two-year master project (ordinarily,
the time needed for development of one product) was completed
in eighteen months and spawned eleven new products.

When management of the purpose-driven organization
sets a general vision and then cascades plans for each segment
of the organization, people become oriented to the future. They
respect the past, but they direct their efforts toward improvement. In effect, they live in a state of constructive discontent,
realizing the difference between the vision and what exists.
"Alignment around a shared vision and purpose is now a recognized characteristic of the creative organization," says Willis
Harman (1987, p. 9).

Sharing Information. Creativity does not happen from
nothing even when people are motivated to create something
new. It occurs when they are in a position to explore and manip-
ulate information. It occurs when they can analyze a situation
and consider alternatives. Imploring people—even inspiring
them—to be creative accomplishes little if they do not have the
building blocks. The purpose-driven leader does all she or he
can to ensure that people have access to the information they
need: current facts that bear on the situation, what has been
tried before, why it did not work, what has changed since then.
Sometimes they need information available at a higher level or
in another department; the leader must cross over these organizational barriers or eliminate them.

In one publishing operation, management continually
asked production personnel to reduce typesetting costs. These
people had no idea what their typesetting costs were or what
caused them. A new manager, who did not have the information
himself, arranged to get typesetting cost data; he passed it along
to key people in the department. This general data showed the
monthly trends in costs. It did not, however, show what the ingredients behind these figures were. So he obtained more detailed
information, which he passed down the line. Then his people

could see what procedures caused unnecessarily high costs. They began to change their operation accordingly, and within six months, they reduced costs by more than 30 percent. Eventually, this manager had to present his people with more data that showed how their activities were affecting other costs because their enthusiasm for reducing typesetting costs was beginning to create undue costs elsewhere. Sharing information is a never-ending process that channels people's quest for improvement.

Openness to Minor Failures. A popular myth says, "Innovative organizations require people who have a high risk-taking orientation." Believing this, management at many organizations tries to encourage people to take high risks. Extensive research by McClelland and his colleagues (McClelland, 1976; Atkinson, 1964) shows, to the contrary, that entrepreneurial people are moderate, not high, risk takers. The research suggests that achievers are driven more by the likelihood of success itself than the consequences of success. The organization that creates conditions that appeal to moderate risk taking stands a better chance of drawing out people's ideas and their commitment to implementation. Innovative people seek an environment where there is challenge and where attainment is truly possible. It is not enough to know that failure is acceptable; there must be a reasonable chance for success. People are not going to be innovative if failure is likely even though accepted. They may leave the organization to find an environment that will increase the chance for success.

The manager who is truly committed to purpose realizes that little is to be gained toward serving that purpose if he wastes time blaming people when new ideas do not work out. Such a purpose-driven manager is more concerned with finding what is wrong or what is missing than who is at fault. Similarly, the manager who builds an organization capable of innovation does not engage in second-guessing, which is often a means of protecting one's turf or authority. Second-guessing implies that the senior person regards only himself as committed, informed, and smart enough to make good decisions. This practice soon discourages others from offering suggestions.

When managers approve an innovative step, they do not merely permit it; they also commit themselves to it. Lack of management commitment can hardly be expected to generate commitment on the part of those involved in the implementation. One company with a long record of failures with new ventures made a practice of making modest investments, assigning a person to work part time on a new project, and allowing a trial period to see if the venture would pay off before making a further commitment. The persons charged with implementation were *assigned;* they were not *enrolled* in a vision of what could be. There was no vision, only a hope for profit. When things broke down, those charged with implementing change felt no sense of failure and no gain in wisdom. They simply slipped back into their routines.

Appropriate Resource Allocation. The company that repeatedly failed to commit itself to innovation despite its attempts at new ventures demonstrates still another requirement for innovation: appropriate allocation of resources. Corporate purpose helps management allocate resources to support those activities that are most important to the organization as it defines itself and its future. Capital and other resources are not unlimited; therefore, management must adhere to priorities. Thus purpose lays out a master framework for innovation.

Down the line, people need resources to carry out the responsibilities for which they are accountable. Sometimes, however, the resources are not available. When their requests for resources are turned down, they can appreciate why if they understand the organization's purpose and are given the facts regarding all the demands for resources. In such cases, they are more apt to seek alternative ways to meet their responsibilities or negotiate a change in expectations rather than to take the denial of resources as a signal to do nothing.

Filling the Key Innovation Roles. A set of roles that foster successful innovation exists. Staffing a purpose-driven organization begins with identifying those roles and assessing the availability of people who can perform them.

At times the leader may fill all the roles. Or each role may be filled by a specific individual. The extent of the dispersal of these roles will vary with the size and complexity of the organization and its activities. But the leader ensures that each role is filled either by a person dedicated to that role full time or by a person filling two or more roles.

Alan Frohman (1974) has identified five key roles in innovation.

Gatekeeper: This person collects and channels information about changes in the technical environment. He stays current with events and ideas through personal contacts, professional meetings, and news media. When the gatekeeper finds relevant information, he sends it to the appropriate person or unit for follow-up.

Idea generator: This role involves the analysis of the information about new technologies, products, or procedures in order to yield a new idea for the company. The fresh idea may be an innovative solution to an existing problem in product or business development or identification of a new opportunity for the organization to exploit in the marketplace.

Champion: The champion, committed to the new idea, advocates and pushes for it. This role involves obtaining and applying the resources and staff to demonstrate the feasibility of the idea. The champion is concerned about results, not risk, and does not spend time studying the consequences of failure. His mission is to remove obstacles.

Project manager: Someone has to draw up schedules and budgets; arrange periodic information sessions and status reports; coordinate labor, equipment, and other resources; and monitor progress against the plan. She integrates and administers the tasks, people, and physical resources necessary to move an idea into practice.

Coach: This function addresses the technical and interpersonal aspects of the work in the innovation process. The coach provides technical training relating to new developments and helps people work together effectively. Because of the variety of subject matter to be dealt with, different individuals at different times may act as coach and the organization may have more than one coach at a time.

Positive View of Technology. Investments in technology to create new products generally signal an innovative company. But investments in technologies for production and distribution may or may not be a plus. Managers often use technology to strengthen their control. "The strategy for productivity improvement has been to develop technology and to design systems that require a minimum of personal commitment from workers, and then to ensure that they put in that minimum by providing multiple layers of supervision and tight systems for controlling costs, quality, and output," observes Roger Harrison (1987, p. 5).

For most of industrial history, technology has replaced physical labor with mental labor. People put into a servant relationship to technology were expected to toil, not create. Corporate executives who see technology as something to trade off against employees are inclined to substitute technology for people—or, at least, people's skills—as they strive to reduce costs and increase their own control. "Many technically driven people move toward automation of machines or information because, as they see it, people have not been able to cooperate and integrate very well. Their response is to take advantage of the new technology and take people out of the equation," believes Dan Ciampa (1988, p. 47). Shoshana Zuboff (1988, p. 390) agrees: "The promise of automation seemed to exert a magnetic force, a seduction that promised to fulfill a dream of perfect control."

Now, however, executives are learning that they cannot fully exploit some of the new technologies unless they have competent people working in the right relationships with one another. In addition, as labor costs shrink to a minor percentage of total costs and the need to deliver value to the customer becomes more critical, many managers have to change their basis for justifying investments in new technology. They operate in a new stage of industrialization. Although they can still choose to use technology to remove employees or tighten their controls on them, they have the better option of reducing the controls that stand in the way of creating greater value. Managers can free people to think and create in an integrated organization. Although they can still automate jobs in which people work like automatons, they can now unleash what people really have to offer: the ability to sense others' needs, make value judgments, and create new methods, products, and services. They have the opportunity to turn to a more positive thrust for technology—for extending the powers of the mind and linking minds in common action.

Technology is throwing open the doors to the development of new skills and abilities that generate value for customers and, at the same time, make the process more fulfilling for workers and more deserving of their commitment. Technology offers the opportunity to open the organization for further innovation. It can shift the organizational climate from controlling to creative. It can allow an organization to leap beyond the innovation embodied in automated machines to the seemingly endless innovation that can come from committed people using technologies that enhance their capabilities.

Commitment to purpose prompts top management to actively examine all the available and relevant technologies and guides its selection of new technology. When the corporate purpose includes employees among the people it serves, it directs technology in ways that maximize what people can do. Without such a guiding purpose, an organization may easily select the wrong technologies or specific technologies for the wrong reasons. Corporate purpose also helps create acceptance down the line for appropriate new technology because people understand that it will help them serve their purpose, especially when they are involved in the selection, installation, and improvement of it. We can see then that the more technology depends on the human factor (and unleashes it), the more it depends on people being linked to an overarching purpose.

Providing Appropriate Rewards. Many managers have been led to believe that the greater the reward, the greater the pace of innovation. Although companies interested in accelerating their rate of innovation often try to establish climates that would appeal to gamblers, research shows that achievers are attracted more by the likelihood of success than the rewards for success. Gamblers respond to the promise of big payoffs, but achievers are stirred to action by the provision of resources that improve their probability of success. The innovative company's budgets, plans, and compensation systems are geared toward making everyone an achiever rather than catering to a few high rollers.

The "pay-for-ideas" technique many companies have used can flush out new ideas from a lethargic organization from time to time, but it will not sustain an ongoing generation of ideas or guarantee successful implementation of those ideas. One of the most effective incentives to innovation comes from outside the realm of financial compensation. It comes from the opportunity to serve one's purpose in daily work. Working with managers who share a vision and information and provide feedback on performance determines, to a large degree, the flow of ideas and people's commitment to implement them. Leaders who advance purpose through others give them credit for acting creatively even when they have to point out that a particular idea is inappropriate. Leaders provide guidance and information so that creative energies flow toward serving the corporate purpose. Managers who are highly visible and accessible to their associates give them something that can be more meaningful than money—they give themselves. Inspired and informed people are a better source of innovation than those who merely have high salaries.

The purpose-driven organization is, by definition, an innovation-seeking enterprise because it defines the gap between what is and what it wants—a gap that can be spanned only by appropriate innovations. It succeeds at innovation because it provides vision, information, resources, and feedback to drive it toward its purpose.

⸮⸮⸮⸮⸮⸮⸮⸮⸮⸮⸮⸮⸮⸮⸮⸮⸮⸮⸮⸮⸮⸮⸮⸮⸮⸮⸮⸮

Chapter 8

Promoting Passionate Leadership

"I say . . . I believe . . . I care . . . I will . . . I'm convinced": These are the words of leaders. They reflect two character- istics—purpose and passion—that distinguish leaders from others and open organizations to constant improvement.

In this era of participative management, you might assume there is less and less room for someone to stand up and say, "Here is where we are going." To the contrary, business or- ganizations need leadership more than ever. The more the command-and-control model erodes, the more organizations will need true leadership at the top and more leaders down the line. They need leaders who can usher in structural change that will provide for continual improvement in effectiveness. The more participative organizations become and the more they get em- ployees committed to the corporate purpose, the more they need leadership at all levels. Fortunately, the changes in structure that are beginning to take shape permit leadership to emerge as never before in corporate history.

The purpose-driven organization begins with an indi- vidual who passionately embraces certain values and defines a vision of where the organization should go and the general means of getting there. This top executive moves the organization to the purposeful stage out of a conviction that meets his or her personal purpose. An organization will not become truly pur- pose driven without leadership to initiate setting a purpose, writing a purpose statement, and designing the supporting con-

113

trol and rewards systems. Corporate purpose needs the vitality and energy that can come only from personal purpose.

However, purpose and passion are not likely to show up among the primary characteristics most of us would list for the millions of managers in whose hands we have entrusted business. To a large degree, management has come to be regarded as a body of technique. In a speech at the dedication of a graduate management center in his name at Claremont Graduate School, October 21, 1987, Peter Drucker warned: "Management . . . cannot be technique alone; it cannot be concerned solely with results and performance. Precisely because the object of management is a human community held together by the work bond for a common purpose, management always deals with the nature of man. . . . That means that there have to be values, commitment, convictions in management, yes, even passion."

We have "neglected the visionary, pathfinding part of the managing process over the last 20 years," says Harold Leavitt (1986, p. 72). *Pathfinding,* according to Leavitt, is that aspect of managing that deals with mission, purpose, and vision as contrasted with the problem-solving and implementation aspects that have received so much emphasis in recent decades. It has been shoved aside by strategic planning and scientific management. Yet as Leavitt points out, "Without some overarching human purpose to steer by, even the best planning and the most skillful implementing can leave organizations spinning in endless circles" (p. 219).

Envisioning the Future

Managing the leap from purpose statement to purpose-driven action depends on the leader's ability to crystalize and communicate values and expectations in a vision that others can easily grasp. "The sense of purpose is not specific enough to form a basis for action; it is necessary to create a vision," says Willis Harman (1988, p. 166). People need to see where they are, where they are going, and why. The purposeful leader clearly and continually attends to this need, and she succeeds because what she wants is what they also want. "Leadership . . . is . . .

inseparable from followers' needs and goals," James MacGregor Burns has observed (1978, p. 19). Michael Maccoby adds that "the leader should be the focus of people's ideals and objectives, to bring out the best in them" (1981, p. 168).

We have found that executives who want to create powerful, adaptive organizations begin the process by looking deeply within themselves. They know who they are and what they want their organizations to be. When they set forth a vision, it comes from a conviction that meets their basic need for purpose-driven action. Because of this deep commitment, they are open to changing the way they perceive themselves. Their challenge is not to become something different but to clarify who they really are. They then have a basis for defining *forward* and *progress*. This enables them to build organizations that know who they are. From that knowledge come meaningful corporate strategy and tactics. Above all, leadership involves envisioning a desirable future and enabling others to get there.

The forward reach of an organization depends on how the people in it perceive the need for change. Both the vision the leader sets out for them and the enthusiasm with which he conveys it create a gap between what is and what could be. From this comes the desire to create change. The leader makes sense of the external environment and judges the organization's strengths against it. The leader can collect, crystalize, and convey a purpose that wins commitment from others if he understands the business environment and the practices that will work for the people in a particular organization. A leader learns what works, what members of the organization find meaningful, and what the customer wants. Visions come from within and from outside, says Thomas Peters (1987). They must be inspiring, clear, and challenging while making sense in the marketplace.

"What distinguishes the leader from the misleader are his goals," says Drucker (1988, p. 14). According to Abraham Zalesnik, "Managers tend to adopt impersonal, if not passive, attitudes toward goals. Managerial goals arise out of necessities rather than desires" (1977, p. 72). We can see then that the role of management is becoming more personal, as well as rational and systematic. Managers no longer need to try to detach themselves from their emotions and values. They will need more inner direction and power than they did when managing the status quo was sufficient. At the same time, it is becoming more and more acceptable for them to express their values and beliefs in the workplace. They can be subjective and take a stand. In the coming years this visionary aspect of management will become more important as organizations find their untapped source of power lies in vision and values that serve continually as a frame of reference against which committed people can compare their actions and ideas.

Taking a Stand

The new leadership that is taking form blends assertiveness with participation. When setting the purpose and vision, the leader welcomes the inputs of others. This openness might suggest that the leader must sort through the values of the organization's members and select the lowest, common denominator values, but what he or she really does is uncover the most powerful ones. Then the leader takes a stand and says, "These are the things that count in this organization."

Taking a stand does not mean that the leader must transform the entire organization and all the individuals in it. Leaders do not make people. Changing people's values is not what leadership is all about. Leaders' honest engagement in discussing values and beliefs with others in organizations can reveal a vision that is already shared, although not clearly expressed. Purpose-driven leaders bring out what is already there. They change not what is inside but what comes out. They uncover what people are committed to or will commit themselves to. They transform not people but the way they are organized and focused. As Warren Bennis and Burt Nanus have observed, "Leaders articulate and define what has previously remained implicit or unsaid; then they invent images, metaphors, and models that provide a focus for new attention" (1985, p. 39).

The new president of one large insurance company spent much of his first year touring the firm's offices around the country and discussing vision and values with employees at all levels.

"It isn't easy to talk philosophy," he admits, "but it gets easier the second time around." He was surprised and pleased to find a great deal of similarity in the things people valued and the type of company with which they wanted to be associated.

Leaders let it be known that they are taking a risk in setting out to fulfill the vision. By virtue of setting boundaries on the field of play with a purpose statement, they exclude certain opportunities from the start. The company will run risks because it has chosen to pass up certain technologies, products, markets, and strategies. Purpose-driven organizations are built by leaders whose dedication to a purpose gives them the courage to take reasonable risks.

Developing a Guidance System

Purpose-driven organizations need leaders who are so passionate about fulfilling their purpose they are willing to experiment with new organizational cultures and styles. Corporate culture became a popular subject for study during the 1980s as a result of the quest for greater effectiveness and efficiency. But little has been accomplished in defining it, much less in learning how to deal with it. We do not believe you change culture by trying to change it. Culture changes in response to something. The way to bring about change in culture is to actively, aggressively, and clearly define the corporate purpose. Establish what the organization is all about, and the culture will define itself around that.

Culture has often been described as behavior-shaping elements such as rituals, myths, heroes, and symbolic leaders. Unfortunately, most notions of corporate culture add up to descriptions of "Here's how we do it; here's where we've been." John Sculley, president of Apple Computer, asserts that "instead of giving us a vocabulary of action, culture limits us by an emphasis on tradition, on yesterday's heroes, on myths, and rituals whose sole value is that they derive from an earlier time.

"In popular use, 'culture' is a closed system; its language is descriptive, and so it misses evidence of action and change. Anthropological categories like 'heroes,' 'myths,' and so on are static," says Sculley (1987, p. 318). He introduces the concept of genetic coding in an organization: Traditional companies "see the future as an extension of the past." In contrast, the emerging form of companies "invent their own future with only a genetic code reference to their past. . . . Genetic coding imprints notions of identity and values as culture does, but in so doing suggests a sense of forward-looking, a sense that everything done today is an investment in the future, not an expression of the past" (p. 319).

Purpose-driven leaders' roles in developing a guidance system go well beyond providing written statements. They work in many ways toward making the organization purposeful by word and action. They insist that decisions be consistent with the purpose, and they ensure that the systems, procedures, and management practices down the line support the corporate purpose. With the proper communications, reinforcing systems, procedures, and style, such leaders show people how the organization's continual shifts in tactics fit within an overall direction.

The major focus of top management should be communicating and adhering to the purpose. This means that managers have to develop an organization-wide set of processes and systems that express, drive, support, and reward actions consistent with the purpose. Top management then has to champion the implementation of these processes and systems through line management and staff operations. When it finds a mechanism or system is working against efforts to serve the purpose, it has to correct the problem. A new idea for a product requires a champion to nurture its development; the same is true for nurturing a purpose.

When there is no stated corporate purpose, leaders down the line may want to fashion a purpose statement for their units of the organization. They may or may not succeed. The chances of thereby creating a purpose-driven suborganization will depend on fitting within top management's intentions, which may shift from time to time. Corporate systems and controls are likely to work against the purpose such leaders are trying to establish. Members of their units may find excitement and power in working toward the purpose leaders set, but then realize that they cannot get the resources from top management necessary to support their efforts. They may even find that the more "successful" they are, the more they are working at cross-purposes with the parent organization. They may be regarded as a nuisance, at best, or a detriment to the overall operation. However, a successful, purpose-driven unit may be just what top management needs to encourage it to make a commitment to creating a purpose-driven organization.

Even when an organization has a purpose statement, it may not be operating purposefully. In one company that created and communicated a new purpose statement, nothing happened to change behavior during the several weeks that followed dissemination of the statement to all employees. Finally, the top management team realized it needed to support written communications with actions that would demonstrate the reality and importance of the purpose statement. One by one, the company's top managers began changing the systems and procedures that governed the scope and pace of people's activities. The president started that process when he put together a team of representatives from several departments to analyze the company's strengths and weaknesses in operations and compare them with similar operations in other companies to establish benchmarks for excellence. In producing the mission statement, the management team had defined the business the company wanted to be in. The list of strengths and weaknesses showed, however, that the company lacked certain capabilities needed to compete successfully in that business. It also highlighted certain capabilities that were irrelevant. That set the stage for developing training programs, acquiring some new equipment, and spinning off certain operations that were not contributing to the company's mission.

The purpose statement asserted the company's commitment to the customer. As he studied the statement, the vice president for sales realized he had to give his salespeople more information on cost, production schedules, manufacturing capabilities, and upcoming products so they could respond better to customers' needs. He began developing closer relations with the product design department so that together they could anticipate and prepare for changes in the marketplace. He also assigned a team to study warehouse locations with an eye toward maximizing responsiveness to incoming orders.

Another vice president established a program to give all of the workers in the manufacturing department hourly raises as they acquired new skills. This provided incentive to reach beyond one's job level to become more flexible. He and several middle managers, engineers, and blue-collar employees began visiting suppliers to share production plans, quality requirements, cost targets, and ideas for speeding the flow of incoming goods.

As the top management team got caught up in building the strengths needed to serve the purpose, they became attentive to selecting people for promotion on the basis of skills and adaptability rather than seniority or conformity. Increasingly, people throughout the company could see that the purpose statement fit the environment—that it was consistent with the signs around them that indicated what "really counts around here." They responded to incentives for doing things that served the purpose. In time, they needed fewer and fewer controls as their commitment to the mission became the best of all control systems.

Building a Foundation for Trust

Because purpose-driven leaders expect other people to control their own activities, the foundation for whatever style or styles they employ is mutual trust. "Trust is the conviction that the leader means what he says. It is a belief in something very old-fashioned called 'integrity.' Effective leadership . . . is based primarily on being consistent," says Peter Drucker (1988, p. 14). Consistency is established in the leader's stand and focus. When they are clear, people will accept "inconsistencies," minor changes in course, and even failures.

Trust opens the door to change. Trust in a major element—the purpose—enables people to accept change in small things and to yield in minor matters of style ranging from how they dress to how they carry out their tasks. It empowers them to do their best and in turn enables their leader to devote attention to the complexities in and around the organization. Today's need for fast, simultaneous decision making requires networking and less hierarchy; that means people must be more trusting than under the old organizational style, which clearly spelled out lines of responsibility and authority.

Leaders receive people's trust partly because they hold a positive view of people. In effect, they embrace Douglas McGregor's Theory Y view that people want to work and contribute to the organization. They are confident that people have potential that has not yet been fully tapped. They operate in the realm of possibility. As a result, they bring the best people to an organization and bring the best out of people.

Because leaders have a genuinely positive view of others, they are willing to share responsibility. They are willing to enroll others in the planning steps that refine the corporate purpose and in identifying the opportunities and problems along the way. They design jobs with a positive, unlimited view of people. They create organizations in which people exercise personal responsibility because they respect each other. Leaders enable others to make greater accomplishments than they have ever expected of themselves.

Purpose-driven leaders are trusted because they demonstrate a high level of selflessness. Because their purpose includes serving others, other people are likely to enroll in it. Purpose-driven leaders are more compelled to serve the purpose than to serve their own egos. Facing a complex environment, conflicting market and technological pressures, and demands for short-term results and long-term viability, leaders realize they need the help of others to deal with uncertainty and ambiguity. They depend on others to offer the best information and advice they can. By contrast, leaders with a selfish purpose that has little appeal to others are likely to cause employees to work at cross-purposes with them.

When leaders take a stand, describe their vision, set out the ground rules, and promise support, they begin building the foundation for trust. Through action and word, they let it be known that they want change, that they will listen, and that they will act on ideas of merit. Because purpose-driven leaders encourage divergent thinking, people trust that they can offer their ideas without placing themselves in jeopardy.

Leaders are single minded about serving the corporate purpose, but they are broad minded about finding ways to serve it. "Where managers act to limit choices, leaders work in the opposite direction, to develop fresh approaches," Zalesnik points out (1977, p. 72). They are passionate about making the changes necessary to attain their purpose. They go all out to involve others in setting strategy and planning because they bring to the organization a new assumption: Everybody has the potential to be creative. They count on people to find new ways to make positive contributions. They are tolerant of people's differences but intolerant of their indifference. They do not like to see people performing below capacity, so they do what they can to improve performance. Purpose-driven leaders make it known that raising questions and offering new answers are acceptable, desirable, and healthy behaviors.

Purpose-driven leaders are so passionate about major objectives that they are willing to make minor changes in their own behavior in order to be more effective through their organizations. They are not afraid to admit what they do not know. They admit mistakes and work quickly to correct them while driving toward their purpose. As leaders at all levels clear away unnecessary corporate hurdles and interferences and provide the necessary resources to get the work done, they show that it is more important for people to be able to serve the purpose than for them to adhere to outdated plans and structures. In too many organizations, managers are concerned more about sticking to a "plan" and obeying the rules than they are about results in the real world. They create bureaucracies that measure activities rather than results. In the purpose-driven organization, leaders are results oriented and place meaningful action above the rules. They change the rules to fit the purpose.

Leaders are not overly concerned about their management style. To them, style is not an act. It is genuinely driven by the purpose. Style is important to the extent that it communicates the purpose and supports its implementation. Rather than worrying about developing or simulating a collection of leadership traits, they focus on drawing on their personal purpose. They do not pause to consider whether they are being leaders. Committed to a purpose they can be passionate about— a purpose larger than themselves—they produce the results of leadership. And that is what counts.

Unfreezing the Organization

We have often heard people associate leadership with inspiring others—winning through charisma. However, not all leaders have charisma. Not all are effective in large groups. Not all are effective in one-to-one relationships. The sole sign of a good leader is whether that person can change the course of others' lives by appealing to their intrinsic motivations. Research on the subject indicates that leadership can occur without charisma being a factor.

Leaders focus people's efforts on a common goal; they give others a vision of a possible future. To do this, the leader needs not only a variety of management skills but also passion. The truly great leader has a high emotional content in what she does. A blend of facts and fire permits the leader to sense the significance of certain technological developments and shifts in people's needs. The passion with which the leader works toward her vision and acts on her values serves as a model, showing people that they can get excited about the job to be done. It assures others that if they put their commitment into gear, the leader is committed to providing needed resources and clearing the way for change. It fuels the excitement—even fun—of testing skills and applying creativity to daily work.

Managers fight fires. In contrast, leaders light fires. With their passion, they unfreeze their organizations so change can occur. They create change while maintaining whatever stability is purposeful. Managers or administrators can handle only stability well. Most managers say, "I want to be comfortable and control things." The purpose-driven leader says, "Let's find excitement in trying new things together. Let's make change a way of life." Most managers say, "Make change and be done with it." The leader says, "Let's build an organization that continually seeks change.'' Most managers say, ''I want quick answers.'' The leader says, ''Keep the questions coming so we won't be blindsided by unexpected events.''

Visible Management

Even with the written word—the purpose statement—and the right systems and structures in place, trust in leaders depends heavily on their personal contact with people. The more visible leaders are, the better they can clarify corporate intentions, the current situation, and a group's performance. In turn, close contact with people throughout the organization is one way leaders can learn about the internal situation, pick up observations about external factors, and determine where misperceptions about the purpose may be occurring. Management must stick near the action to keep attention focused on the purpose. Absence does not ''make the heart grow fonder'' in organizational life. People will quickly forget printed statements, and systems and structures can drift away from emphasizing the purpose. Management's primary role is to make sure the purpose comes alive and stays alive.

Thomas Peters and Robert Waterman (1982) popularized the term *management by walking about* (MBWA) in their book, *In Search of Excellence.* They stressed the value of managers at all levels moving around and listening to employees. By no means is MBWA a matter of snooping around to keep people in line. It is the reverse. It means setting things in motion. Simply wandering around the plant or office is not sufficient. MBWA has to be done with purpose. It is done to reinforce purpose. The manager has to know who she is going to see and what that person's projects and priorities are. She can then help the person focus on what needs to be done. MBWA is not a popularity contest.

Managers can build relationships that are trusting and effective by sharing information about what the company is doing well and what it is doing poorly. Perhaps even more importantly, MBWA is an opportunity to share feelings, values, and vision. It gives employees a firsthand look at the consistency between the leader's intention and his behavior. It is an opportunity to build trust as people witness their leader sticking to his purpose and resisting a short-term solution that does not fit the corporate purpose.

MBWA does not mean getting out and telling people what to do and how to do it. Trusting and trusted leaders have no reason to pretend that they have all the information or that they must hoard it.

Direct contact is perhaps the best way to handle a key part of the leader's job: setting expectations and tracking performance. Setting expectations involves defining departmental and individual goals that are consistent with those of the organization and then arriving at mutually acceptable expectations for performance. This process results in a commitment from the individual based on understanding the big picture and how he or she fits in. Some people may not have had any clear expectations of themselves before. Or they may have had only selfish, short-term expectations. Managers may be surprised to learn how much people want an explanation of how corporate purpose translates into day-to-day expectations for them. The following list indicates what the purpose-driven leader attends to in order to let people know where the organization should go and how it is doing:

- Making a personal conviction to a purpose
- Stating a corporate purpose
- Communicating that purpose again and again
- Communicating it through all structures and systems
- Demonstrating willingness to change in order to serve the purpose
- Listening to suggestions for change
- Effecting change by empowering others
- Explaining how the changes serve the purpose

Walking about provides a means of letting people know one-on-one what their manager thinks is important through the subjects he discusses and the questions he asks. And because the purposeful manager believes these people are important and can make a difference, he steps aside and lets them get the work done. We have heard more than one manager say, "All I have to do is keep out of people's way."

This is the other side of the MBWA coin—management by stepping aside (MBSA). After the manager sets the direction, he gets out of people's way so they can get moving. It takes courage and trust to operate in this hands-on/hands-off fashion. But it works when all parties trust that they are working toward the same purpose and that each has the information and resources needed to fulfill his or her responsibilities. The manager shows that he is deeply interested in the work left in employees' hands and that he trusts them to execute it in keeping with the corporate purpose. Employees want and need openness, feedback, and the sharing of values so they can operate "on their own" (Pascarella, 1987).

While managers are generally eager to learn so they can get ahead, leaders establish a learning environment so others can make a growing contribution to the organization. Leaders not only provide information but also enable people to seek information for themselves on customers, competitors, and their own organization's capabilities. When people perform well, purpose-driven leaders feel successful. Leadership largely involves the growth of others. Leaders build people's confidence in themselves and in the organization, nurture their competence, and help them uncover talents. In direct contact with individuals, leaders can convince them that they can make a difference.

While the flow of information, inspiration, and feedback encourages people to follow leaders, it also generates leadership in others. The environment in which potential leaders find themselves has a great deal to do with their development into leaders. Nothing creates leaders like proximity to a leader. Purpose-driven leadership at the top of an organization brings forth purpose that in turn brings out the leadership abilities of others. This environment nurtures leadership as more people take charge of their own activities with the power and direction of the corporate purpose reinforcing their personal purpose.

Although the ranks of management seem overcrowded, there has been a perennial shortage of business leaders. Troubled top executives ask, "Where will we find the leaders we need? Can we develop them? If so, how?" These executives sometimes fear that they themselves lack the leadership ability needed to start the change process, and they are troubled by the shortage of leadership down the line to support them. Because most organizations are structured to maintain stability and control, they block the development of the sort of leadership needed to generate change.

Once a leader steps forth to establish a purpose-driven organization, however, the search for leaders becomes less troublesome. As purpose flows from top management through all the layers of management and into the ranks of all employees, leaders surface everywhere. People who have a vision of the future and know they can help shape it will take that future into their own hands.

Chapter 9

〜〜〜〜〜〜〜〜〜〜〜〜〜〜〜〜〜〜〜〜〜〜〜〜〜〜〜

Dealing with
Managerial Paradoxes

Textbooks define *management* as a planning, administering, and controlling function. A manager's primary responsibility has generally been to keep the system "under control." Yet, on the job, things are seldom under control. A manager constantly risks upsetting the balance of interests among the many people who have a stake in the organization: investors, employees, customers, suppliers, and the public. The manager's job is to maintain order. But one group's interests may conflict with another's. And each group is apt to change over time. How can a manager be expected to maintain order?

A manager has to conduct a balancing act in dealing with things that always seem to be paired in opposites. The job seems to be one of finding *the* right answer in situations that pose more than one right answer, no clearly right answer, or an answer that will solve one problem and create others.

The leader who is driven by purpose is not intimidated by the incompatible opportunities and activities she faces in a complex and tumultuous world. She deals successfully with numerous paradoxes because she puts them into the perspective of how each relates to the purpose. Purpose provides the central reference for resolving what would appear as paradoxes to others, enabling her to do what is consistent—consistent in terms of always serving the purpose. It helps determine what not to do— those things that might be desirable ends in themselves but do not clearly serve the corporate purpose. The following six paradoxical pairs are among those a leader must handle.

Balancing short-term considerations with the investment of time and resources needed for long-term payoffs: Purpose helps determine which short-term opportunities support long-term objectives by providing the resources or positioning that will enable the organization to move onward.

Balancing the need for innovation as well as the demands for stability and control: Purpose helps determine what is worth changing and what is worth preserving. Change and stability are opposites, but purpose-driven leaders can look at both squarely and draw upon each to move toward their purpose.

Dealing with both tangible and intangible considerations: If the corporate purpose covers both financial matters and human values, then leaders look beyond physical resources and see value in the intangibles presented by people and information. They can see that some of their company's facilities, for example, should be kept in place while others should be sold. They are not wedded to the facilities as some managers might be; leaders are committed to the purpose and see facilities only in terms of how well they serve that purpose.

Being "soft" and "hard" in the treatment of people: Unless part of the corporate purpose is to retain all present employees, a manager may at times choose to sever relationships. He does so not because he does not value people but because he values the commitment he and others have made to serve the purpose, which may be centered on serving people. Commitment to purpose helps leaders deal with emotional issues such as firing people when the good of the organization is at stake. The power of their commitment to purpose helps overcome emotional resistance to an unpleasant task. Purpose then enables a person to do things that "scientific" managers decide to do but sometimes cannot do.

Satisfying demands of external parties, which are often in conflict with internal demands: If the purpose statement includes consideration of everyone interested in the organization, purpose-driven leaders do not work to create winners and losers; they strive for results that will benefit everyone over the long term. They do not regard their organization as a separate, self-contained entity; they work to remove barriers between the "inside" and "outside." In the years ahead, effective organizations will blend input from customers, suppliers, and others with that of people inside the organization.

Seeing that quality and cost reductions are not necessarily trade-offs: Because leaders are committed to quality as part of their corporate purpose and because they must also operate a financially successful enterprise to remain in business to deliver quality, they do not see these factors as an either/or proposition. Companies that made quality their number one objective have found that they have been more effective at cost reduction than when they concentrated on cost reduction alone.

Growing concern for quality and serving customers have challenged traditional corporate purpose—or the lack of it. These interests are becoming the cornerstone for corporate purpose. They are prompting a change in mind-set among business leaders. They are learning that quality may be more than a set of numbers—that all qualitative concepts cannot be reduced to quantitative factors. Their work today demands that they attend to intangible as well as tangible factors, the realities of human aspirations as well as those of the marketplace. Those who are driven by purpose turn paradoxes into possibilities and possibilities into realities.

The purpose-driven leader deals with the paradoxes from which others retreat because he recognizes the possibilities the paradox offers. Rather than seeing situations in terms of either/or, he finds and/both solutions. He sees complementary pieces of a puzzle. "A paradox may signal an inadequacy in the way we are looking at a question," says Timothy Ferris (1988, p. 356). The purpose-driven leader has a better way of looking at questions because he begins thinking with his purpose in mind and seeks alternatives to get there. He is not dedicated to tradition or the easiest route.

Purposeful leaders work in the realm of possibility, stepping out with a vision of the future. From that vantage point, they can see new possibilities that can serve the vision. For them, "impossible" is an opinion, not a fact. Management is often challenged, for example, to attend to things other than the bottom line. Conventional managers are likely to respond, "Sorry, but we have to be profitable first." Purpose-driven leaders find that they can serve human values and still create a good bottom line. By tending to two or more considerations simultaneously, they sometimes reach solutions that are far better than normal expectations. For example, involving employees by meeting individuals' needs for recognition, growth, learning, and belonging can also enhance the organization's quality and productivity far beyond the old control methods of improvement.

Purpose-driven leaders not only deal with paradoxes but also operate in a manner that looks paradoxical:

> They are intuitive and artful as well as rational and scientific.
> They work directly with people down the line while also delegating responsibility.
> They show concern for others while firing poor performers or downsizing an organization to make it more effective.
> They participate at times and stand back at other times.

The purpose-driven leader may operate in a manner that defies the either/or mandates of traditional management because he has stated what really counts. This makes it legitimate (and effective) to do things in his daily routine that may seem inconsistent. He works directly with people to ensure that they understand the corporate purpose, makes available the information they need for solving problems, and checks on their need for resources. At the same time, he delegates the execution of the work to be done because he knows he cannot do everyone's job better than he or she can.

Because the leader is committed to purpose that requires all-out effort from others, he shows concern for them. He looks after their well-being and enables them to develop new skills. That same commitment leads him to fire employees whose performance is below standard or reduce the size of the organization, if necessary, to enable it to serve its purpose. He willingly shares power and information that have traditionally been the marks of success because he derives his sense of success from the organization's progress toward its purpose, which is inextricably tied to his personal purpose.

The purpose-driven leader may vary his style from time to time, depending on the circumstances. He uses a participative management approach, for example, in some, but not all, situations. When people see him clearly serving the corporate purpose, they can accept the varying styles. What might look like paradoxical behavior is not. The corporate purpose states what the results of style must be and what values it should respect, but the purpose does not dictate style.

What Scientific Thinking Really Means

The passion and purpose of the men and women we describe in this book run counter to the reason and rationality long regarded as attributes of "good managers." Such concepts as values and vision seem to have little place in an era of computer printouts and cost justification. They are not the products of rational, analytical thinking. Vision is arrived at intuitively; when others accept it, they do so intuitively. Taking a stand that commits the organization to a direction and operating procedures without a guarantee of success is largely not a rational action. Participative management opposes management's fundamental concept of control. We can see the power of purpose and passion when they are in action, but they do not fit with scientific management precepts. We are used to controlling and analyzing, not enabling others or using intuition.

Is the ground swell of management toward purpose and passion a departure from the scientific management that drove American industry to greatness? Could purpose-driven management undermine all that has proven useful in management techniques? Understandably, some people construe the emphasis on the human, or "soft," factors as signaling the end of the use of quantitative, analytical methods in guiding business organizations. Leaders who are dedicated to the new mission and methods of management may feel apologetic about breaking with the past. Even though they are convinced they are doing the right things, they cannot always quantify and prove their results in conventional business terms.

The techniques themselves are not being left behind; only the context in which they are used is being challenged. The conventional management mind-set is being criticized for its ineffectiveness. For years, management has struggled to be scientific as it strove for predictability and control. It studied factors of success and tried to establish formulas for replicating it. Scientific management reached its zenith in the late 1970s. At the same time, interest in the soft factors was mounting; they seemed to be worthy not only as ends in themselves but also as the means to better financial performance. Ironically, scientific management's cool, calculating analysis of financial factors was failing to produce success even in financial terms.

Challenges to the analytical, calculating nature of the business world are not new to the "scientific" manager. But the ultimate challenge to the assumptions on which management has based its mission and methods now comes from science itself. A closer look at what *scientific* really means reveals that purpose and passion are most appropriate. Despite appearances to the contrary, we are not witnessing the end of scientific management. Purpose-driven leadership runs counter only to old notions of what scientific methodology is—and to outdated concepts about the nature of the world. It is very much in harmony with the scientific method and with new views of the world.

Nowhere has management "science" strayed farther from science than in its method of thinking. From the start, its proponents failed to embrace the full range of thought processes that would make it fully scientific. "Scientific management" has been the capstone of over three centuries of elevating rational thought processes over the irrational and reducing aspects of business into understandable and controllable components. It flourished in a society that assumed *scientific* meant rational, calculating, and analytical thought processes only. People who embraced it overlooked the fact that scientific advances come as a result of intuitive leaps, which may later be supported by experimentation and reasoning. They regarded those who use their intuitive powers as the exception rather than the norm; they tolerated creative people under certain conditions and watched them carefully at all times.

This simple, static view of the world led managers to search for precision, order, and certainty. They assumed that if they could screen out emotion and intuition, then they would scientifically find the way to get the job done most efficiently. This led to segmenting work into tasks, dividing management activities into functional specialties, isolating business from the rest of the world, and differentiating one's work life from one's personal life. Being "scientific" meant managers should deal only with what could be quantified, but this assumption ran counter to people's rising concern for quality. As a result, many organizations fell out of step with what the marketplace wanted from the organization and what the work force offered it.

While the quantitative analytical approach works well for defining a problem and marshaling facts, it does not facilitate innovation. Scientists know that the more complex the problem, the better the intuitive approach suits it. The rational, empirical approach does not help managers deal with attitudes, beliefs, and feelings. That is why business leaders are discovering that they need to balance the mechanical skills of rationality with intuitive ways of cutting through the complexities of this computer age.

According to Roger Harrison, one reason intuitive thinking has not been "legitimate" in organizations "is that many of us have trouble distinguishing high-quality intuition from sloppy, wishful thinking. . . . Intuition is not a substitute for facts, for experience, or for logic. It is a way of building on and going beyond facts and experience. Studies of high-performing individuals in many fields have shown that successful people tend to visualize the results they want in their lives and work. . . . Rather than planning in detail what they will do and how they will go about it, they start by creating an intensely alive mental representation of the end state" (1983, p. 216).

Answering the need to create organizations that can deliver innovation will depend on making "management science" more truly scientific. This means using not only intuitive power but also human emotions. The creative act is driven by emotions. Leadership and followership are largely matters of emotions. When people commit themselves to a purpose, they are addressing their central beliefs and feelings. They then want to use their ability to generate and implement ideas. To tap this power, some leaders turn their attention to concepts that defy quantification: culture, values, vision, commitment, and new organizational relationships. Ironically, we will find that the more results-oriented management becomes, the more it will be driven by values and visions. But management's attention to human factors does not have to end in abandoning all that was good in its old techniques. Successful leaders will demonstrate that being scientific and being human are one and the same.

Lessons for Business from Science

Science offers leaders valuable lessons about how to think and about the nature of the world in which they pursue their purpose. New observations and theories in physics, biology, psychology, and mathematics challenge the simple sketches of reality we have drawn from the scattered signals we receive through our senses. If we want to be truly scientific in our managing, we should heed the new findings of science and update our views of the world. We can learn a great deal from nature's paradoxes.

Uncertainty. When some of today's managers were in school, they were taught that the material world was made up of electrons, protons, and neutrons. Since then, the number of identified subatomic particles has proliferated, and scientists theorize that matter is not matter, but energy—or both—or neither. Deep in the subatomic realm, physicists find that the smallest bits of matter behave as both particles and waves of energy—a paradox if there ever was one! What we have are not rock-solid building blocks, but abstractions.

With relativity theory and quantum theory, twentieth-century physicists have offered us uncertainty, not the machine-like certainty of earlier times. When some experiments showed subatomic units behaving as particles and other showed them behaving as waves, Niels Bohr offered a resolution of this apparent paradox. His concept of ''complementarity'' allowed that both notions are correct; what we see depends on which experiment we conduct. The world is too complex to be explained fully in the simple models of reality we construct.

Physics, perhaps the strictest, most exacting of the sciences, has led the way in breaking down the certainties long associated with science. Today's physics deals in probabilities. According to Werner Heisenberg's ''uncertainty principle,'' for example, the more we know about the location of a particle, the less we know about its velocity and vice versa: a paradox.

In organizations, people tend to view one another as having fixed roles. The manager concerned primarily with a subordinate's presence—her simply being there from 9 to 5—disregards the worker's motivation and aspirations. The truly modern leader treats people as forms of energy rather than as physical ''particles,'' as something less definite and possessing virtually unlimited potential. Business leadership can raise its effectiveness if it recognizes that it is not dealing with absolutes and learns to live with uncertainties and paradoxes.

Relationships. Subatomic ''particles'' act as patterns of energy inextricably bound up in relationships to one another. They seem to ''know'' instantly when something happens elsewhere in the universe. They seem to be separate entities and somehow have unity at the same time: another paradox. Some scientists conclude that there may be no particles at all—that all ''things'' may be part of an organic web of relationships.

Similarly, we can view organizations of people as sets of relationships, not merely as collections of discrete particles. Organizations often are made up of good people who are rendered ineffective because of the relationships and policies we impose on them. The organization is often its own worst enemy. Organizational charts reflect only probabilities about an individual's responsibilities and relationships in today's complex and changing organizations. We cannot judge a person's ''velocity'' (power and talent) by his or her location on a chart. Organizations generally attempt to limit the number and scope of formal relationships an individual may have. The people who get things done, however, often operate outside the lines on the organization's chart. They know how to use the informal networks to produce results when the formal structure gets in the way.

Even the corporation itself is not a discrete particle vis-à-vis the rest of the world; it is a set of relationships among owners, employees, suppliers, customers, and the public. Science would instruct us to view the organization in terms of its many relationships. It suggests to business leaders the need to seek quality in all the company's endeavors as a response to people's fundamental drive to honor their relationships with one another. Many management problems come down to a matter of communication because organizations are made up of people trying to express their relationships.

The Observer's Influence. Scientists have learned that the observer cannot remove herself from what she is studying. A person cannot observe a phenomenon without having some influence on it. The observer is separate yet a part of what is going on: still another paradox. Similarly, corporate culture cannot be separated from leadership. The leader has a relationship to the organization's culture and an impact on it. To a large degree, management has had a negative effect on organizations' culture by robbing organizations of their vitality. Managers sometimes have behaved in ways that resemble an atom in an excited state. When an atom is excited, an electron has absorbed some additional energy and moved to a higher orbit. Similarly, in an organization, a person who is manipulating his or her own upward progress may be stealing energy from others. That person moves to a higher orbit at the expense of the well-being of the whole.

When an atom returns to its ground state, it gives off radiation as the electron moves down an orbit. There is a parallel in the organization that is flattened by reducing the number of levels in its hierarchy so power can be dispersed. Some managers have found they can generate a quantum leap in organizational effectiveness by sharing power rather than hoarding it. They involve more people in finding, defining, and solving problems, and they are able to implement strategies more effectively than autocratic managers can.

A Shift in Paradigms

Because we cannot fully comprehend reality, we construct models—*paradigms*—to represent the world. The "great machine" paradigm is now being undermined as science advances. Scientists tell us there is more to the world than we have seen and far too much for any one model to capture.

The worldview basis of American management culture comes from the line of thinking that viewed the physical world as a great machine separate from the intangible world of the mind. More than three centuries ago, René Descartes asserted that the emerging science for studying the physical world was not suited for all human studies. This dualism of physical and spiritual realms eventually led to the separation of science, technology, and later management from religion and philosophy. It seemed to legitimize the uncoupling of human actions and values. A manager was a master mechanic of the mechanical world.

Along the way, we forgot that the things science deals with do not constitute the whole world. The paradigm under which American management developed was grounded largely in the physical realm, but it is crumbling as another paradigm emerges. The new one holds that the mind and body—the spiritual and physical worlds—are very much related; they may be one and the same.

The new paradigm restores value to other-than-rational ways of knowing long displaced by those who have misused science. Rather than breaking things down into smaller and smaller components in order to study and manage them, this new paradigm values synthesis, which brings things together into a bigger picture. The time is right for the purpose-driven leader who brings disparate things together into a vision and then produces results.

Harnessing Purpose-Driven Chaos

If managers expect order in a mechanical universe, it is understandable that they will seek control and predictability. Control worked to improve organizational effectiveness in the past. Organizations got by with people not knowing where the organization was going, but today they need the help of committed and competent people. Because economics, technology, and our view of the world have undergone profound changes, managers now find themselves keepers of a system that is less and less appropriate in what it strives to do and how it goes about it.

Recent experience in the workplace shows that flexibility and learning are often more effective than controls. More managers are abandoning notions of control and are exploring more powerful ways of bringing people's talents to bear on the corporate purpose. Some of them are deliberately stripping away the controls of hierarchy and autocracy. As they substitute purpose for control, they are creating what may look like chaos but might better be called purpose-driven chaos. The new model of reality is prompting them to create new, more effective approaches to management such as the following examples:

- Seeking *contribution* from people rather than *trying to control* them
- Nurturing *creativity* rather than forcing *compliance*
- Seeing oneself as *coaching* players rather than *commanding* troops
- Unleashing *commitment* rather than settling for *consent*
- Building a sense of *community* instead of forcing *confinement* of individuals from one another or isolating the organization from the rest of the world
- Generating *cooperation* rather than encouraging internal *competition*
- Accepting *complexity* instead of contriving *certainties*

Management now faces several critical choices in marshaling its people power. It can establish policies and procedures to compel people to do what they are told, or it can demonstrate that it cares about people as whole persons and coach them in their development to be more effective. It can bargain with people to win some temporary consent, or it can build trust and release their commitment. It can browbeat people into compliance, or it can be upbeat with them and unleash their creativity. The organization of the future will be built on coaching, commitment, and creativity, not the absolutes and precision that we thought were being ''scientific.''

∽∿∽∿∽∿∽∿∽∿∽∿∽∿∽∿∽∿∽∿∽∿∽∿∽∿∽∿∽∿∽∿∽∿∽∿

Chapter 10

Involving Others in Purpose-Driven Management

The success of participative management throughout business and other organizations demonstrates that decision-making authority can be dispersed more widely in an organization than it has in the past. It reaffirms that the role of leaders is to manage a process for making decisions rather than making all the decisions themselves. Their job is to get people with the best information to arrive at a high-quality solution and commit themselves to effective implementation.

Organizations that recognize the need for participation by people throughout their ranks are not submissively responding to demands for a say in the workplace. They are not seeking mere cooperation. They want people's commitment to attacking problems and opportunities in every quarter—internal and external. They want to capitalize on each person's special awareness and expertise.

Since the early 1970s, more and more companies have experimented with various forms of involving workers with participation in decision making. In such processes as quality of work life and quality circles, hundreds of thousands of people have learned to define, prioritize, and solve operational problems. What seems to be a movement is not really a movement because it has many forms, and its proponents have various ends in mind. Some use participation to improve the quality of their product or service. Some people turn to it to improve productivity; others use it to improve the quality of working life. Employed properly, participation can deliver all these benefits simultaneously. The net effect of this broad movement has been to open organizations to innovation—to ideas for improvement in the organization's objectives and its practices.

The failures in participative management have occurred especially in cases where management merely imitated the actions of managers in other companies. Some managers lack either the deep conviction that people have something to contribute to the organization or the skills to draw out contributions. Increased attention to the human factors does not mean that all managers have really accepted the required philosophy or acquired the necessary skills. Some have approached it with their traditional skills or intentions. As a result, their encounter with such processes as quality circles or quality of work life has too often been fruitless.

In general, however, the movement toward wider participation has been on the right track. A critical mass of success stories and believers has developed, raising the likelihood of participation soon becoming the rule rather than the exception. A growing number of top executives and middle managers realize that the traditional autocratic style does not produce enough innovation or tap people's energy factors.

Participation and purpose go hand in hand. The purpose of purpose is to align the activities of people throughout the organization; their participation is meaningless, and sometimes harmful, if it has no guidance system. Participation in itself will not meet the organization's needs if people do not know what counts in creating effectiveness. Their diverse efforts to reduce costs or enhance revenues will not add up to long-term success for the organization unless they are focused by some means. In turn, purpose is of little value if people cannot participate in its pursuit.

Because participation is an integral part of purpose-driven management, let's clear away some of the smoke surrounding the subject. Assumptions about employees' participation in decision making range from ill-founded condemnation to unrealistic optimism. Many executives think participative management is an answer to their prayers; others see it as a jungle in which they could get lost. Just what is participative management? Who is a participative manager? When is participative management appropriate?

A number of myths are perpetuated by managers who tried participative management "one time and it didn't work," by those who claim to practice it but whose subordinates do not agree, and by others who see themselves as "paid to make decisions around here."

Myth 1: "Participative management is a human relations approach; it is not results oriented." The case for participative management has been made countless times in improved productivity and better quality. It should not be employed simply to improve relations or morale, although these are often important by-products. It is a means of achieving the organization's desired short- and long-term results. More people become involved in setting targets, determining how to achieve them, resolving problems, and establishing compatible systems and procedures. This involvement in turn fosters widespread acceptance and commitment to achieve the targets.

Contrary to an underlying assumption that supports this myth, not everyone will seize immediately upon the opportunities offered by an open, innovative environment. Nonmanagement people may not know how to participate; they are used to being told what to do, when to do it, and how to do it. Managers and supervisors may be reluctant to give up the power and status they derive from the status quo; they have to be shown that power will be measured in terms of *results*.

Myth 2: "Real managers don't manage participatively." Involving others in decision making threatens the "I'm in charge" self-image of many managers. They think participation means they have to give up responsibility. Quite the contrary! Participative management can unleash responsibility of others without diminishing managers' responsibility.

Seasoned participative managers realize that the most effective form of control is the control subordinates exercise on themselves. Participative managers have found that they can rely on these internal controls when they give people the opportunity to exercise their responsibility, encourage their involvement in decisions that will affect them, allow them to develop their talents, and let them know where they stand relative to expectations. Consequently, workable participative management means they have to waste less time devising external controls. They can concentrate on nurturing creativity rather than trying to impose control, a big responsibility.

Myth 3: "Participative management is a management 'style.'" This approach to management is more than a matter of presentation or appearance. Its substance includes such elements as setting goals, planning actions, tracking performances, two-way communication, support, resolving conflicts, training, and development. The manager who attempts to participate without mastering these hard business activities would merely be affecting a style—one that is unlikely to deliver results that serve the corporate purpose. The manager who is concerned with being participative at all times probably has his eye more on style than on results.

Myth 4: "Participative management is democracy in the workplace." Democracy and participative management are not the same thing. Although they both solicit ideas from constituents, there are differences in the way they do so. Democracies rely either on direct vote by persons with equal power and rights or on a representative system that in effect gives everyone a voice on every issue. Participative management attends to the differences in individuals' talents, levels of information, and decision-making skills. Participative organizations have tiers of decision making; individuals are involved in defining and solving problems where they can make a meaningful contribution to maximum effectiveness of the whole or some part of it. The definition of effectiveness of the whole is determined in the establishment of purpose and vision—something that is done by a few who consider the interests of many. Participation does not mean that everyone votes on every major corporate issue.

Myth 5: "Participative management involves a lot of meetings." This statement has some validity. Participative management does involve interaction and exchanges of ideas that group meetings can enhance. But meetings should be called only when necessary to serve a specific purpose. This myth may be due in part to the fact that managers who lack skills in meeting leadership conduct meetings that are typically not productive. As a result, they call more and more meetings, thereby causing frustration for all concerned. The most productive meetings in a purpose-driven environment are sometimes the spontaneous ones—the unscheduled hallway or water-cooler conversations in which people experience the fun, excitement, and immediacy of sharing ideas.

Myth 6: "Participative management is not applicable at the higher levels." This misguided view exists for two basic reasons. First, the proliferation of participation programs for hourly workers and first-level supervisors has been well publicized. Thus from the literature it is easy to infer that these programs are applicable only at lower levels. Second, it is much easier to see room for improvement in someone else's approach to decision making than your own. Higher-level executives may exhort lower levels to be more collaborative without recognizing the value of following their own advice. This may, in turn, explain the frequent failure of such programs. Lower-level managers do not have supervisors who practice what they preach; they have no models to follow.

A participative management approach can address the need for greater coordination, information sharing, and problem solving by people at any organizational level. Certainly one of the most appropriate places for participation is among top executives when they are setting corporate strategy and allocating resources. The president of an industrial automation firm stated the situation well, "With the awesome global competition, we have to try to be sharper in setting our strategy and assessing our marketplace than others. It is imperative that I create our competitive advantage through participation and idea exchange at the top."

Myth 7: "Participative management is easy." Perhaps the assumption that this management approach is merely a style oriented toward building human relations leads some managers to assume that all they have to do is act the role of "Mr. Nice Guy." Implementation can be far more challenging than that for at least two reasons. First, it requires skills in areas that are not traditionally familiar to many managers—interactive goal setting and problem solving, team building, and peer management, to name a few. Most managers need to develop these skills before they venture into participative management.

Second, participative management, as with any other management approach, must be compatible with and supported by other aspects of the organization. Good leadership is not enough; the total organizational environment must support it. The leader has to align planning and budgeting procedures, reporting systems, personnel policies, reward systems, and other organizational factors with the participative approach and with one another for the organization to run smoothly.

Myth 8: "Participative management works in any organization at any time." This myth, like the previous one, is overly optimistic. Managers who are successful with participative management treat it as one tool among many from which they can choose. They know when it is appropriate to use it. They approach it seriously and with a willingness to figure out how and when it can be applied more effectively than other approaches. They realize, for example, that some situations require speedy decisions or the presentation of nonnegotiable directions and are not suited for participation.

In addition, some managers prefer to give orders, make their own decisions, and hold the reins close to their chests. For them, participative management is an unnatural act. This does not mean they do not get results; rather it means their choice of management tools is more limited, and they are not likely to get the best results in all situations. Some organizations similarly are not ready for this management approach. Their procedures, policies, and culture are not conducive to participation. Even in paternalistic organizations, where people are treated humanely, managers may have little experience in treating people in ways that fully tap their resources.

Give-and-Take in Management

There is a time to sell, a time to tell, and a time to rely on the participation of others. Effective leaders use all three tools in making decisions. To be consistently purposeful, leaders find that a participative mode is appropriate at some times and not at others. Purpose-driven management may appear contradictory or paradoxical, but its consistency lies in its substance rather than its style.

Managers who know when to employ participation have three sets of management tools to draw on: give, give-and-take, and participative. Managers use the first, give, when they tell their subordinates what to do without asking for their input. These givens are not negotiable. They are usually specific conditions or goals that must be satisfied for the good of the organization. Give management works best when the manager has special information or technical knowledge that enables her to best determine the direction, when the manager is unwilling to consider other approaches, when time does not permit discussion, and when others have little interest or need to be consulted. Give management is often used to present overall direction. For example, top management is usually expected to state the purpose of an organization. Many people believe top management's job is to supply direction.

Most managers are practical enough that they weigh the anticipated reaction of their subordinates in arriving at givens. They present the givens to help their people focus on and perform tasks. They are not trying to assert their authority or force compliance.

When managers use give-and-take management, the second set of tools, they first make a tentative decision or plan and then present it to subordinates. They outline the problem so others can question, comment, and offer alternatives. They solicit give-and-take discussions to explore and test for better ideas before making a final decision.

Managers find that give-and-take works best when subordinates have relevant information. They recognize that a discussion will contribute to a better decision than if they made it by themselves. Some managers assume that give-and-take is simply a matter of selling a decision in a one-way deal, but they are wrong. It involves giving and taking in an open-minded search for the best thinking. The elements of time pressure and subordinates' interest and expectations must be compatible with exercising this management approach.

When they use the third set of tools, participative management, managers rely on subordinates to help define the issues and the responses. They turn to participative management in situations where they believe superior performance is more likely to result from their subordinates' ideas and views. Thus they do whatever they can to heighten contributions by others.

Participative management does not eliminate the manager's role or reduce her accountability for results. Rather it requires much greater attention to soliciting ideas, encouraging discussion, integrating diverse input, and managing a group. It works well when subordinates have substantial information and knowledge about the situation in question. It is not likely to be the best approach if there are urgencies; a manager may have to do things quickly without consulting others.

Success depends on managers' skills such as the ability to conduct productive meetings, lead group problem solving, and mediate differences constructively. It also depends on the manager's willingness and readiness to involve others. If her mind is made up about a decision, or she sees no value in seeking others' ideas, then involvement of others is spurious. Rather than court frustration and disaster, she should pick another management approach that will help her and her subordinates get positive results.

Profile of Participative Managers

Participative managers are not permissive, meeting-happy cheerleaders. They do not try to accommodate others at the expense of results that contribute to the corporate purpose. They develop management skills that foster commitment, high-quality work, and superior results. They strive for competence, not contentment. In our close observations of several top-level executives who practice participation, we find they have seven essential characteristics in common.

1. They have a clear understanding of the purpose and direction of the organization. Written purpose and direction statements give people in an organization focus, targets, and hills to charge. Participative managers recognize this fact and communicate the organization's purpose. They set significant and relevant priorities and limits in the context of the organization's purpose and goals. This gives their employees jobs with meaning beyond the job descriptions. It also gives them reason to recognize their interdependence with others.

Donald Petersen, chief executive officer of Ford Motor Company, exemplifies how some top executives value corporate purpose. Referring to his company's "Mission, Values, and General Principle" statement, he told us, "We want this statement to be to Ford and all its employees around the world a basic platform on which we all stand together. Our goal is to have everyone in the company understand and embrace what this statement means, what is behind it, and what we should be doing to live the values and guiding principles. I see the guiding principles as a code of conduct. They tell us how to do our jobs, how to behave toward one another and towards our customers, dealers, and suppliers. They remind us of what is expected of us and what we should demand of ourselves."

Joe Gregory, president of Perfection Corporation, a major producer of fabricated pipe products, explained to us that he believes that participative management "starts with a clear picture of what the company is trying to accomplish. With this, a participative manager has a sense of where he is going and then uses participative methods to get a lot of input on how to get there."

2. Participative managers have high-performance expectations of themselves and others. These participative managers emphasize their expectations and ensure that standards of performance are clearly stated for everyone. Eric Mittelstadt, chief executive officer of GMF Robotics, says he encourages subordinates "to set their hurdles high. Invariably, they will set them higher or smarter than I would." The participative managers we have observed are realistic. They believe people will be motivated to achieve high goals that they have a hand in setting or at least influencing. They also recognize that the people who must achieve these goals are in the best position to know the roadblocks and shortcuts. Therefore they let others influence their own goals and performance standards, while expecting them to take reasonable risks.

Donald Petersen sees it this way: "When I say 'risk taking,' I'm not talking about a Las Vegas roll of the dice. I'm talking about reasoned judgment—judgment that doesn't require every issue to be studied to the point of total exhaustion. When you worry an issue to death, you've closed your options. It's easy to say no. But winners in the risk-taking business are those who know when to say yes."

3. *They demonstrate the ability to use participative management or other approaches, depending on the situation.* These leaders know that blindly following management theories or personal preferences rarely provides a productive response to actual circumstances. Rather, they base their actions on an asessment and understanding of what is going on at the time. They read such things as the business climate and the organization's ground rules. These factors indicate the relative advantages and disadvantages of giving orders, using the give-and-take approach, or relying on participative management to deal with a particular situation. William Hoglund, executive vice president of General Motors, points out that "anyone who is good with participative management realizes it applies only some of the time. Sometimes I have to tell my people we don't have time to talk about this decision. But I have to be good at picking when I operate this way."

These participative executives also know their subordinates. Recognizing that no two people are alike, they think in terms of individuals rather than a mass of people. They have learned that some persons need a great amount of structure and frequent feedback while others perform better with more freedom and independence. Joe Gregory notes that "when some people dig in their heels, I stop and try to figure out where I might have been wrong. With others I realize it is not necessary to react that way."

Self-understanding is another factor in determining whether to use give management, give-and-take management, or participative management. These corporate leaders understand themselves—their needs, pressures, and biases in a particular situation. For example, if they know clearly what they want their subordinates to do, they will tell them. They will not try to disguise their solutions under a participative mask.

Eric Mittelstadt says, "Effective management is a balancing of all approaches in order to get results. This means a participative manager must exercise his option to make the selection." William Hoglund agrees: "One of the most important and hardest skills of participative management is to know when not to use it."

4. Participative managers are to be accountable for results. These leaders know they are being paid for their subordinates' achievement of results consistent with the organization's goals. How they manage is up to them within constraints set by the organization. If subordinates are not performing well, they reassess the situation and change their approach. They know that the use of participation does not let them off the hook for results. The buck still stops with them. They believe a sure sign of a manager who does not accept accountability is someone who blames subordinates for "lack of motivation" or "unwillingness to change." A participative manager sees his job as harnessing and channeling people's energy.

Because these executives hold themselves accountable for results, tracking and reporting performance are critical to the way they operate. They realize that conditions change, plans and goals may have been misunderstood, and unanticipated events occur. That is why they want a continual flow of timely, accurate, and relevant information from a purpose-driven tracking system that will permit them to readdress a situation quickly and effectively. Joe Gregory says, "One of my most important tools as a participative manager is our financial reports. They tell me what to discuss with my team." William Hoglund adds, "Some managers get confused. They try to manage numbers and report people. To be successful, you have to manage people and report numbers."

5. They use two-way communication. For participative managers, two-way communication is an absolute must. First of all, exchanging ideas and sharing information can improve on the ideas of one person. Second, if managers truly accept accountability for group achievement, they want their people to be informed and understand what they are told so they can perform well. Third, participative managers recognize that their role in communication does not end with sending the message. Communication is incomplete until the receiver understands the message. Therefore, above all, participative managers are skillful listeners. As Donald Petersen says, "We need less emphasis on having all of the answers and more on being sure we ask the right questions." Participative managers constantly strive to keep people informed of the good news and the bad, encourage questions and ideas from others, and ask questions to make sure that the message is getting through.

Eric Mittelstadt describes himself as "forceful" at times—a trait he does not see at odds with participative management. He tries to "remind people after I have had my say that I still need their input and ideas—that my ideas are not a substitute for their good judgment. Probably the most important thing I do when I get ideas better than my own is to state out loud that I am changing my mind. For participative management to work, I must be open and willing to admit I don't always have the best idea."

6. *They use group methods and interpersonal skills.* Appropriate use of group problem-solving, decision-making, conflict-management, and meeting-leadership skills are indispensable tools for these participative managers. They conduct effective, productive meetings as a matter of efficiency. They believe it wastes time to deal with each person individually in matters common to all. They regard meetings as opportunities to prompt two-way communication among all the participants and stimulate creativity.

"If a manager calls a meeting, he must know how to set the climate to make it productive," says Eric Mittelstadt. "I have seen too many meetings where people come together and there has been no planning or preparation. That is not participation; that's stupidity. Group process skills and sensitivity to know when to use them and when not to use them are important to a participative manager. I have to be careful to recognize when to convene my staff and when to meet individually with people."

Participation does not require managers to put everything to a vote. They may let people have their say before a final decision is reached, but they themselves determine how much influence they exert on their group. Their major building blocks for participative management are skills for managing differences, leading meetings, and building interpersonal relations. A manager cannot be truly participative without these skills. Simply assembling people into a group, for example, does not automatically endow them with the ability to work together effectively. They are no more a team than is a collection of basketball players meeting on the court for the first time. Ford considers interpersonal skills and teamwork so important that it includes them as criteria to be evaluated in reviews of managers' performances.

7. *They trust people.* Perhaps the most distinguishing attribute of these participative managers is their willingness to trust, to demonstrate confidence in others' ability to perform. They regard trust as the currency they exchange for people's initiative, responsibility, and best effort. They depend on trust to focus people's efforts on performance rather than preservation of the status quo. Trust allows for openness, questioning, creativity, and commitment—the essentials that managers need for sustaining a corporate purpose.

A purpose-driven organization constantly demonstrates to people that they are trusted. They in turn trust the organization to use a number of accepted means to help them serve their individual and collective purposes. There are times when they accept givens. On other occasions, they are eager to participate in making choices. In either case, they are committed to give all they have.

Assessing Your Skills

Table 3 will help you rate your characteristics as a participative manager. Profile yourself by answering the self-view section in Table 3. Then get feedback from subordinates. Next, examine the gaps for each characteristic between now and how you would like to be in the future. Develop a plan to close the

Table 3. Your Profile as a Participative Manager.

Participative Management Characteristic	Self-View		Subordinates' Feedback	
	How I see myself now	How I'd like to be	How my subs see me now	How they'd like me to be
1. Clear understanding of purpose and direction of organization.	1 2 3 4 5	1 2 3 4 5	1 2 3 4 5	1 2 3 4 5
2. High-performance expectations of self and others.	1 2 3 4 5	1 2 3 4 5	1 2 3 4 5	1 2 3 4 5
3. Ability to use participative management or other approaches, depending on situation.	1 2 3 4 5	1 2 3 4 5	1 2 3 4 5	1 2 3 4 5
4. Willing to be accountable for results.	1 2 3 4 5	1 2 3 4 5	1 2 3 4 5	1 2 3 4 5
5. Use of two-way communication.	1 2 3 4 5	1 2 3 4 5	1 2 3 4 5	1 2 3 4 5
6. Use of group methods.	1 2 3 4 5	1 2 3 4 5	1 2 3 4 5	1 2 3 4 5
7. Trust in others.	1 2 3 4 5	1 2 3 4 5	1 2 3 4 5	1 2 3 4 5

Point values: 1 = Not at all. 2 = A little. 3 = Fair amount. 4 = Quite a bit. 5 = All the time.

gaps and review it with subordinates. Finally, solicit feedback regularly. We have used this profile method to help top executives and middle managers look at some of their characteristics and skills and then ask their subordinates to rate them on these factors.

As we have said, we do not advocate using participative management techniques for all occasions. The decision to use give, give-and-take, or participative management depends on the specific activity and the persons with whom you are dealing. We offer Table 4 to suggest the degree of participation to use for a variety of management activities and people in various organizational levels.

Table 4. What Works Best?

| | Management Approach to | | |
| | Top | Middle | Lower |
Activity	Organizational Level		
Defining organization's purpose or mission	PM	G	G
Setting organization's strategies and resource allocation	PM	G&T	G
Setting department-level goals and plans	PM	PM	G
Preparing operating plans and budgets	PM	G&T	G
Setting individual-performance targets	G&T	G&T	G&T
Establishing performance criteria and standards	G&T	G&T	G&T
Preparing individual action plans	PM	PM	PM
Managing routine stable operations	G	G	G
Fostering creativity	PM	PM	PM
Conducting problem-solving meetings	PM	PM	PM

PM—Participative management
G—Give management
G&T—Give-and-take management

Purpose and Participation Require Patience

Even purpose-driven leaders who allow participation by others will find that they need a great deal of patience to see their organization become truly purpose driven. It takes a long time—usually several years—for an ongoing organization to significantly strengthen its purposefulness.

One large consumer goods company, about to make major changes that encompassed many of the concepts outlined in this book, projected it would take at least five years for full implementation. This organization has 2,700 employees in four U.S. locations. The president of a small service firm with 100 employees and six branch offices reported that, after two years, he is beginning to see the impact of efforts to become more purpose driven. The president of a multibillion-dollar industrial company told us, "Realistically, it will take at least seven to ten years for the reorientation and revitalization of our outfit. The engine that drove us to where we are now can't be shut down overnight nor should it be. To uproot unnecessary past practices and replace them with purposeful ones takes careful digging." A fourth organization, with 850 employees, set expectations with them regarding the time frame for implementing a plan to become more purpose driven. They agreed that two to three years was the minimum.

The job of creating a purpose-driven organization is never finished. Top management must constantly watch the evolution and maintenance of the purpose. It has to monitor ongoing activities—both strategic and tactical—and evaluate the emergence of new activities to ensure that purpose is being served. (See the Resource, which follows this chapter, for guidelines for assessment.) Management measures *results* to see if the organization is really competitive and if it is accomplishing the goals set in the purpose statement, strategy, and plans. Equally important, managers recognize that people are vital to the organization's success and therefore check *their perceptions* regarding what the organization is doing and how it is performing. They value what others think about the purpose and the way the organization is or is not serving its purpose.

In Chapter Six, we described the tracking systems that are necessary to monitor the effectiveness of executing plans—plans framed by the purpose. But top management has to be sure that the tracking system itself is doing the proper job.

Management needs to ask itself and others questions that cover the entire range of being purpose driven: establishing and communicating a purpose, generating a strategy and plans that bring it to life, tracking the appropriateness of the plans and their execution, and rewarding behavior that serves the purpose. The tracking system does not put an organization on automatic pilot. Leadership at the top has to focus its attention continually on the total challenge of being purpose driven.

It takes patience to pursue the suggestions we have presented in this book. It takes time to unfreeze, move, and refreeze patterns and practices in any organization. Quick fixes will not give root to anything meaningful or long term and certainly not accomplish what we are advocating.

Becoming more purpose driven is within the realm and reach of many organizations. Some are taking deliberate steps in this direction. But breaking some of the chains of Stage Three structure, policies, and routine takes a great deal of time. Being purpose driven involves carefully choosing the areas in which to spur change while reinforcing areas where goals, plans, and activities are already consistent with the purpose. This is the paradoxical nature of effective purpose-driven leadership.

Resource: How to Gauge Your Organization's Purposefulness

Success in increasing purposefulness depends heavily on the understanding, acceptance, and commitment of people inside and outside the organization. As we said in Chapter Five, energy factors move the organization. Therefore, management must know at all times how others regard the organization's success in implementing its purpose-driven strategy. Their collective view needs to be surveyed to indicate (1) progress or change consistent with the purpose, (2) new opportunities for increased effectiveness in implementing the purpose, and (3) weaknesses that can curtail or limit implementation. Management should ask people with a stake in the organization, "How well are we doing compared to how we said we would do?" and "Are there other things we can do to move us toward our purpose?" Surveying is important because top management's perception of the organization's purposefulness and the effectiveness of the support systems may differ from the perception of others for whom the organization intends to be purpose driven. Various groups' perceptions of the organization may differ from top management's view at the outset of the journey to become a purpose-driven organization and at any time in subsequent years.

A survey will perform an additional valuable function: It will remind the organization's members of the importance of the purpose and the need to pay attention to its implementation. The results can be used to stimulate discussion, solve problems and plan actions throughout the organization to keep it growing.

For many managers, this book offers solid and substantive starting points as to what to consider in creating and sustaining a purpose-driven organization. We have devised a list of many questions that will help them review the factors to consider for action. These questions are grouped into categories that relate to each of the major topics in this book.

The questions provide an overview of all aspects of a purpose-driven organization. Each group of questions is headed by a general question that top management should constantly ask itself if it wants purpose to really drive the organization. To learn the answers, top management will have to check periodically on the organization's purpose, plans, tracking, rewards systems, and results. It needs to check on progress toward serving the original intent of the corporate purpose and to determine whether that intent should be updated to reflect major changes in the external environment or other people's values and aspirations.

The detailed questions serve as samples for tailoring a survey of employees and outside parties to gauge their perception of the company's purposefulness at various times. Questions can be selected and modified to fit a specific methodology and the particular group being surveyed. These questions may also suggest points for discussion in interviews with people about the organization's purposefulness. For example, ''What accounting reports and information that you receive tell you how well you and others are implementing your strategy?'' The important point is that the survey should measure or track the relevant elements of the organization's effort to become more purpose driven and to develop information in a form that promotes its discussion and use.

Openness to Improvement

How willing is your organization to adopt new ideas and strategies?

1. Is your organization willing to change?
2. Does your organization stick to what worked before, or is it willing to introduce new programs and actions?

3. Does your organization balance its efforts at reducing costs with investing for its future?
4. Does the organization encourage individual development and learning?
5. To what extent is rocking the boat discouraged?
6. To what extent is your organization caught up in its culture and tradition and missing opportunities to improve?
7. Does the organization recognize and try to respond to the legitimate claims of all relevant parties, including employees, shareholders, and customers?

Establishing a Purpose Statement

Are all the critical elements included in a purpose statement?

1. Does your organization have a statement of purpose?
2. Was the preparation of the purpose statement preceded by addressing the appropriate questions? (See Chapter Three.)
3. Was the purpose statement prepared following these steps?

- Checking top management's commitment
- Outlining the purpose statement's contents and how to develop the necessary data
- Collecting information
- Creating a picture of the future
- Writing a statement
- Testing the purpose statement

4. Does the purpose statement contain a description of the organization's current and future business?
5. Does the statement of purpose contain a section on how the organization should operate internally and tap people's energy factors?

Communicating the Purpose Statement

How well has management promulgated and explained the purpose?

1. Do people throughout the organization understand the purpose and direction?
2. Is the purpose accepted as relevant and meaningful?
3. Does top management show a commitment to the intent and implementation of the purpose statement?
4. Are people at other levels committed to carrying it out?
5. Are there sufficient reminders and reinforcements of the purpose staement through periodic communication?
6. Does the organization take advantage of multiple communication devices for getting the message out?
7. Is the purpose discussed as part of the organization's planning process?
8. Has the purpose statement been presented to relevant external parties?
9. Has the effectiveness of communicating the purpose been measured?
10. Has measuring communication effectiveness been used to strengthen the understanding and clarity of the purpose?

Planning

How do managers set goals and priorities and allocate resources in ways that serve the purpose?

1. Does the planning process follow a top-down pattern with purpose serving as the framework?
2. Does your organization take appropriate advantage of opportunistic planning?
3. Does your organization take suitable advantage of individualistic planning?
4. Does your organization use formal planning and procedures effectively?
5. Does your organization use the best possible mixture of opportunistic, individual, and formal planning?
6. Do your organization's managers recognize and consider the relevant external forces and pressures (technological, economic, regulatory, competitive, marketplace) affecting its business in their decisions?

7. Does your organization recognize and consider the relevant internal factors (for example, proprietary assets, major competitive strengths, and technological strengths) affecting its business in its planning and decision making?
8. To what extent are employees' interests, values, and skills considered during the planning process?
9. Is there appropriate emphasis on planning at all levels?
10. Is the information used in planning timely and valid?
11. To what extent are values considered in planning and in setting strategy?
12. Does management balance its attention to short-term and long-term goals in its planning?
13. Are budgets constructed to meet short- and long-term goals?
14. Do the tactical, day-to-day decisions support the plans?

Tracking

Are procedures for data collection and performance reports accurately gauging performance against the corporate purpose?

1. Does the organization balance attention to external and internal events and trends in its tracking?
2. Does the tracking system monitor and report activities that carry out the philosophy and internal operating section of the purpose statement?
3. Does the tracking system collect and make available from all possible sources the types and amount of information needed?
4. Does the tracking system effectively use formal and informal methods of data collection?
5. Does the cost and accounting information serve the internal needs of the organization as well as external requirements for financial reporting?
6. Does the tracking system use the proper bases of comparison for interpretation of performance?
7. Are the elements of the tracking system (for example, accounting information, performance reports, distribution of information) serving the purpose and plans?

8. Do the accounting procedures and reports adequately cover progress and performance toward long- and short-term goals?
9. Does the organization put the proper emphasis on tracking at all levels?
10. Do the overhead allocation and other accounting methods to cost the product or service support the implementation and tracking of the plans for each unit of the organization?
11. Does the tracking system capture and report activity that builds the human organization?
12. Are performance reports and other tracking information available to all the people who can use them?
13. Does the tracking system provide meaningful and relevant information and analyses?
14. Is the evaluation of individuals' performances related to the primary goals of their unit?

Alignment of Systems and Procedures

Are the numerous policies, procedures, and systems sending consistent messages to serve the corporate purpose?

1. Do the systems and procedures throughout the organization reflect and support the purpose?
2. Do the organization's systems and procedures reflect and support the long-term plans?
3. Do the systems and procedures throughout the organization reflect and support the short-term plans and budgets?
4. Are the goals and priorities for all departments and levels consistent with their purposes?
5. Are the goals and priorities for all departments and levels consistent with each other and integrated with the corporate purpose?
6. To what extent does management try to make systems and procedures compatible and fit together?
7. Does the organization's structure facilitate carrying out the organization's plans?
8. Are the policies of the organization consistent with its plans and objectives?

Communication and Coordination

What is the level of cooperation among people throughout the organization who have to work together?

1. Do managers anticipate coordination requirements and interdependencies when planning work activities?
2. Is there effective lateral coordination in your organization?
3. To what extent do people at different levels cooperate with one another?
4. Does the organization encourage networking and open, multidirectional communication, or does it follow traditional vertical channels only?
5. Are communication procedures in your organization effective?
6. Is communication open and honest, or is it guarded and cautious between levels?
7. Is communication open and honest, or is it guarded and cautious between departments?
8. Do internal communications and day-to-day activity support the organization's purpose and plans?

Rewards

How well does the reward system support the organization's purpose and plans?

1. Do people perceive rewards as being related closely to contributions to achieving plans and the purpose?
2. Are rewards based on what the tracking system captures and reports?
3. Does the reward system recognize short- and long-term achievements?
4. Do the elements of the pay system (merit increases, bonuses, extra compensation) support the purpose and plans?
5. Are employees recognized and rewarded for initiatives and actions in the best interests of long-term objectives and strategies?
6. Are merit increases tied to activities and measures that reflect a unit's plans and priorities?

7. Are promotions perceived as tied to achievement of plans and goals?

External Relations

Are relations between people inside the organization and relevant outside parties purpose driven?

1. Is top management accessible and in contact with relevant people outside the organization?
2. How well does management try to understand what constitutes value in the eyes of the organization's customers?
3. Is the organization receptive to ideas from its customers?
4. Does the organization work with its customers to come up with new ideas and improve its competitive position?
5. Is management receptive to ideas from suppliers?
6. Does the organization work with its suppliers to develop new ideas to improve costs and quality?
7. Does the organization maintain close ties with the community?

Stability

Is the organization using its experience constructively?

1. Does the organization encourage efforts to maintain stability that is consistent with plans?
2. Does management operate with an effective blend of control and flexibility?
3. Does the organization recognize and build on its past successes as well as encourage change when and where appropriate?
4. Do the organization's practices show a balance of memory and vision?

Innovation

What is the climate for encouraging the generation and testing of new ideas?

1. Is management trying to develop a climate that supports new ideas and innovation as opposed to supporting just a few entrepreneurs?
2. Are there specific ways for offering, evaluating, and supporting new ideas?
3. Are modest improvements encouraged or does management only encourage dramatic ideas (for example, home runs)?
4. Do people know where innovation is needed to support the organization's plans and purpose?
5. Is the organization willing to accept minor failures as the price for encouraging innovation?
6. Does management support a moderate (not extreme) level of risk taking?
7. If a new idea appears worthwhile, are adequate resources allocated to check it out?
8. Are there sufficient people in each of the necessary roles (gatekeeper, idea generator, champion, project manager, coach) to pursue new ideas and projects?
9. Are differences of opinion accepted and used constructively?
10. Does the implementation of plans allow room for initiative and judgment to reach the objectives, or is adherence to plans the primary concern?
11. Is there a positive view of technology as offering new routes for the organization to achieve its purpose and plans?
12. Is technology used to "unfreeze" the organization and stimulate additional new ideas?

Management Practices

Are managers' behavior and methods consistent with the organization's purpose and plans?

1. Do managers use management methods (give, give-and-take, and participative) that are most appropriate for each situation?
2. Do managers rely excessively on one management method despite a situation's requirements?

3. Do managers throughout the organization have high expectations of themselves and others?
4. Do managers see themselves as accountable for the results of their work group?
5. Do managers use two-way communication practices?
6. Do employee relations and management practices strive for compliance or for commitment from employees?
7. Do managers use interpersonal skills effectively?
8. Do managers show that they understand the difference between participative and permissive management?
9. How do managers deal with inappropriate behavior and unacceptable performance?
10. Are meetings called when and only when they are needed?
11. Do managers effectively plan and conduct meetings?

Top Management

Is top management providing direction, communication, and support for carrying out the purpose?

1. Does top management champion the purpose of the organization?
2. To what extent is top management passionate in its communication of purpose?
3. Does top management behave in ways that encourage actions that serve the organization's purpose?
4. Is top management willing to set limits and make difficult decisions about resource allocation that are in keeping with the purpose?
5. Is top management accessible and in contact with people inside the organization?
6. Does top management remove roadblocks and stay out of the way of employees who are trying to achieve short- and long-term objectives?
7. Does top management accept and effectively handle the paradoxes of management?
8. Does top management establish and abide by ground rules regarding the ways people are managed and treated?

9. How much confidence and trust does top management show in employees throughout the organization?
10. Does top management admit that it does not have all the answers and seek them from others?
11. Is top management willing to admit mistakes and learn from them?

References

Anthony, R. N. *Planning Control Systems: A Framework for Analysis.* Boston: Division of Research, Graduate School of Business Administration, Harvard University, 1965.

Atkinson, J. W. *An Introduction to Motivation.* New York: D. Van Nostrand, 1964.

Bennis, W., and Nanus, B. *Leaders: The Strategies for Taking Charge.* New York: Harper & Row, 1985.

Block, P. *The Empowered Manager: Positive Political Skills at Work.* San Francisco: Jossey-Bass, 1987.

Burns, J. M. *Leadership.* New York: Harper & Row, 1978.

Cialdini, R. B. *Influence.* New York: William Morrow, 1984.

Ciampa, D. *Manufacturing's New Mandate.* New York: Wiley, 1988.

Davis, S. M. *Managing Corporate Culture.* Cambridge, Mass.: Ballinger, 1984.

Drucker, P. F. *Management: Tasks, Responsibilities, Practices.* New York: Harper & Row, 1973.

Drucker, P. F. "Leadership: More Doing Than Dash." *Wall Street Journal,* Jan. 6, 1988, p. 14.

Ferris, T. *Coming of Age in the Milky Way.* New York: William Morrow, 1988.

Frohman, A. L. "Critical Factors for an Innovative R&D Organization." *The Business Quarterly,* 1974, *39* (4), 72–81.

Frohman, A. L. "Energy Factors: Implementing Your Strategic Plan." In W. D. Guth (ed.), *Handbook of Business Strategy.* Boston: Warren, Gorham & Lamont, 1985.

Harman, W. "Global Mind Change." *Noetic Science Review,* Winter 1987, p. 9.

Harman, W. *Global Mind Change*. Indianapolis: Knowledge Systems, 1988.

Harrison, R. "Strategies for a New Age." *Human Resource Management,* Fall 1983, *22,* 209–235.

Harrison, R. "Harnessing Personal Energy: How Companies Can Inspire Employees." *Organizational Dynamics,* Autumn 1987, *16,* 5–20.

Hayes, R. A. "Strategic Planning—Forward in Reverse?" *Harvard Business Review,* Nov./Dec. 1985, *63,* 111–119.

Hayes, R. A., and Abernathy, W. "Managing Our Way to Economic Decline." *Harvard Business Review,* July/Aug. 1980, *58,* 67–77.

Hiromoto, T. "Another Hidden Edge: Japanese Management Accounting." *Harvard Business Review,* July/Aug. 1988, *66,* 22–26.

Leavitt, H. *Corporate Pathfinders*. Homewood, Ill.: Dow Jones-Irwin, 1986.

Leider, R. J. *The Power of Purpose*. New York: Ballantine, 1985.

McClelland, D. C. *This Achieving Society*. New York: Irvington, 1976.

Maccoby, M. *The Leader*. New York: Simon & Schuster, 1981.

Mintzberg, H. "Crafting Strategy." *Harvard Business Review,* July/Aug. 1987, *65,* 66–75.

"The New Breed of Strategic Planner." *Business Week,* Sept. 17, 1984, pp. 62–68.

Ohmae, K. *The Mind of the Strategist*. New York: McGraw-Hill, 1982.

O'Toole, J. *Vanguard Management*. New York: Doubleday, 1985.

Ouchi, W. *Theory Z: How American Business Can Meet the Japanese Challenge*. Reading, Mass.: Addison-Wesley, 1981.

Pascarella, P. "Management by Stepping Aside." *Industry Week,* June 1, 1987, p. 9.

Pascarella, P., DiBianca, V., and Gioja, L. "The Power of Responsibility." *Industry Week,* Dec. 5, 1988, pp. 41–50.

Peters, T. J. *Thriving on Chaos*. New York: Knopf, 1987.

Peters, T. J., and Waterman, R. H., Jr. *In Search of Excellence*. New York: Harper & Row, 1982.

Potts, M., and Behr, P. *The Leading Edge.* New York: McGraw-Hill, 1987.

Quinn, R. E. *Beyond Rational Management: Mastering the Paradoxes and Competing Demands of High Performance.* San Francisco: Jossey-Bass, 1988.

Sculley, J., with Byrne, J. A. *Odyssey.* New York: Harper & Row, 1987.

Sheridan, J. "Texas Instruments: Looking for 'Easy' Answers." *Industry Week,* May 16, 1988, pp. 66–68.

Thompson, W. N. *Quantitative Research in Public Address and Communication.* New York: Random House, 1967.

Thompson, W. N. *The Process of Persuasion.* New York: Harper & Row, 1975.

Toan, A., Jr. *Using Information to Manage.* New York: Ronald Press, 1968.

Zalesnik, A. "Managers and Leaders: Are They Different?" *Harvard Business Review,* May/June 1977, *55,* 67–78.

Zuboff, S. *In the Age of the Smart Machine.* New York: Basic Books, 1988.

Index